CUSTOMER RELATIONSHIP MANAGEMENT

By

Dr. T. Vetrivel

MBA., M.Phil., PGDCA., Ph.D.

Professor

Department of Management Studies

Velalar College of Engineering & Technology

Thindal, Eorde – 638 012

DISCOVERY PUBLISHING HOUSE PVT. LTD.

NEW DELHI-110 002

Published by:
Tilak Wasan

DISCOVERY PUBLISHING HOUSE PVT. LTD.
4831/24, Prahlad Street, Ansari Road
Darya Ganj, New Delhi-110 002 (India)
Phone: +91-11-23279245, 43764432
Fax: +91-11-23253475
E-mail: parul.wasan@gmail.com
discoverypublishinghouse@gmail.com
web: www.discoverypublishinggroup.com

***First Edition:* 2011**
ISBN: 978-81-8356-877-7

Customer Relationship Management

Printed at:
Shree Balaji Art Press
Delhi

Dedicated to
My Lost Loving
Mother and Father

Preface

This work has been an enjoyable experience. The book provides several review of literature and also provides the practical experiences of Customer Relationship Management (CRM) practices in retailing with Fast Moving Consumer Goods (FMCG). It is hoped that the Research scholars will find this body to be interesting, non-intimidating, and of practical use. This CRM concept has emerged in the recent past. In my twelve years of teaching and research experience, I have had the opportunity to work with various retailers and the customers of Fast Moving Consumer Goods with various issues in the form of research thesis. Moreover, my continuous teaching of this subject and research work enabled me to write this book in a clear and accessible style so as to benefit students, teachers, research scholars and executives of business and public retail organizations.

The text attempts to provide both the theoretical and computational aspects of the subjects as well as a number of practical experiences. The sustained interest among researchers and academicians has resulted in a multifaceted exploration of CRM concepts, including behavioural as well as economic aspects. A number of papers and articles in academic journals as well as business publications, seminars and conferences have helped in disseminating the knowledge and experience. New technologies for distributing and collecting information have affected both companies and customers. Customers are continuously informed about products through different modes of communication.

The CRM highlights the importance of using Information Technology in creating, maintaining and enhancing customer relationships. However, it is not hassles free and there is a need to develop a better understanding of CRM and of how business concerns can use a CRM system to successfully ascend in business by wisely managing the data about the relationship between the customers and the business concern, largely depending upon the data pertaining to a particular business domain and that could be effectively gathered. The IT affects business activities in many different ways. Primarily, it can facilitate communication, information sharing and collaboration processes with customers and within a company or network.

In the Indian market, customers are supposed to be treated as kings, following the business dictum given by the Father of nation Mahathma Gandhi, who pointed out that 'A shopkeeper should not think that he is doing any service to a customer, but he shall always remember that only the customer is doing a service to the shopkeeper by giving him an opportunity to do business with him'. As the nation prospers, and as the business expands with increasing competitiveness among the business players of a business domain this dictum gains more value since such customer-focus would not only fetch more profit but also would infuse some ethics and spirituality in business in the present cut-throat competitive scenario of business.

The research was conducted for a period of three and half years. The period of the study was confined to 2006 to 2009. The first year was spent for collecting the review of literature, and second year was spent to collect the opinion from the retailers and customers. Data analysis and interpretation, correction and finalizing the book were done during the rest of the period.

This book is divided into seven chapters. The *First Chapter* gives the extensive but clear picture of research design, which includes Introduction to CRM, Need for the Study in the retail business domain and in the study area Erode, Statement of the Problem, Objectives of the Study, Hypotheses and Scope of the Study, Period covered by the Study, Limitations of the Study, Research Methodology adopted, and Frame Work of Analysis.

The *Second Chapter* discusses the previous studies relevant to the present research. The *Third Chapter* focuses on the conceptual framework of customer relationship management. The *Fourth Chapter* highlights an overview of the marketing of FMCG products and the progress of FMCG retailers of Erode district. The *Fifth Chapter* covers the ways and means of the FMCG retailers' practicing of CRM and the problems faced by them in the study area using different statistical tools. The *Sixth Chapter* presents the FMCG customers' opinion on CRM practices by the FMCG sector of Erode with suitable analytical calculations and the *Seventh Chapter* recapitulates the key Findings and Conclusion of the study. At the end of this chapter, certain Suggestions have been put forth for better Customer Relationship Management by the FMCG retailers of Erode district.

This book has been written for the students of CRM – MBAs majoring in marketing, faculty offering an elective MBA and M.Phil courses on CRM, Research Scholars and the Retailers those who are interested in the concepts and practice of Customer Relationship Management.

T. VETRIVEL

Acknowledgements

> *A timely help rendered, even if small, is far greater in worth than the whole earth*
>
> – **Thirukkural**

My sincere thanks to Dr. C. Swaminathan, Ph.D. Vice-Chancellor, Bharathiar University, Coimbatore for allowing me to do my research work in this field.

I feel elated in expressing my deep sense of gratitude to my revered guide and supervisor, Dr. A.P. Muthulakshmi, M.Com., M.B.A., M.Phil., Ph.D. Principal, Department of Management Studies, CMS Academy of Management and Technology, Coimbatore, under whose guidance and untiring support, I have completed this work. The stimulating ideas, invaluable suggestions offered by her lead me towards the accomplishment of this book. She not only guided me in the research work, but also, is my motivator, educator and philosopher who guided me in each and every progress of my life. I wholeheartedly thank her for her kindness and support throughout the period of the study.

I deem it a honour and proud privilege to place on record my deep sense of gratitude to Dr. L. Manivannan, M.B.A., Ph.D., D.L.L., PGDCA, Associate Professor, Department of Corporate Secretaryship, Erode Arts College (Autonomous), Erode for his inspiring guidance, valuable suggestions and constant encouragement in the successful completion of this research work. Indeed I am beholden to such a learned professor for his valuable comments and patience of hearing and considering my views at every stage of research work. I genuinely accept that, without his endless support and caring, my dream would not have come true. I sincerely thank him.

I express my sincere thanks to Dr. K.T. Varkey, Ph.D. Principal, CMS College of Science and Commerce, Coimbatore for giving me the permission to carry out my research work in a successful manner. My Special thanks are expressed to Dr. S.Sandhya Menon, Ph.D. Principal, CMS Institute of Management Studies, Chinnavedampatty, Coimbatore for her constant encouragement to complete this research topic.

I also express my heartfull thanks to all my friends of CMS College Faculty Members, especially Prof. S.Rajasekar, M.B.A., M.Phil., (Ph.D)., H.O.D. Department of Business Management, CMS College of Science and Commerce, Coimbatore for their encouragement and cooperation to complete my research.

I wish to express my deepest gratitude to my late mother Tmt. K.R.Jayanthi, and my late father Thiru. K.G.Thiyagarajan, for their love and support and all sacrifices they have made throughout their life. They have taught me the principles and values that have guided my life. Their extraordinary foresight and courage to send me for better education, has allowed me to pursue my successful career and profession. This thesis is dedicated to my beloved parents.

I am very grateful to the Management of Velalar College of Engineering and Technology, Particularly to Mr. S.D.Chandrasekar, B.A. Secretary, Dr. P. Sabapathy, Ph.D. Administrative Director, and Dr. K.Palanisamy, Ph.D. Principal for permitting me to pursue with this research work and all my faculty colleagues for their moral support extended to me.

My sincere thanks to Dr. D. Muruganandam, M.B.A., Ph.D. Director, Department of Management Studies, MPNMJ Engineering College, Erode, for his valuable guidance and providing all the facilities required for executing this research work, and who had been a source of great inspiration and unparalleled guidance right from the initiation of my research work.

I express my sincere thanks to Prof. D. Vijayadurai, M.A., (Ph.D)., Associate Professor, Department of English, Chikkaya Naiker College of Atrs & Science, Erode for giving me the confidence and offered the novel approaches and ideas in preparing my research thesis.

I express my heartfull thanks to all my friends especially, Dr. P. Komarasamy, M.B.A., M.Phil., Ph.D. Assistant Professor, Department of Management Studies, Nandha Arts College, Erode for their kind cooperation and timely help for analyzing the data towards the completion of this work.

My sincere thank to Mr. B. Sivakumar, MLIS., M.Phil., Librarian, and Mr. M.Chandrasekar, BLIS., Assistant Librarian, P.S.G. Institute of Management, Coimbatore for the continuous and constant help for providing valuable books and journals. I also thank to the Library Authorities of Alagappa University, Karaikudi and Kongu Engineering College, Perundurai for permitting me to take the references, magazines and journals to go in a right way to develop of my research work.

Words are inadequate to express my gratitude to the number of Retailers of Erode District, who readily and graciously took time to provide all the data required for this work. This thesis would not have seen the light of the day if it had not been thoroughly proof-read, corrected and polished with appropriate expressions by Prof. P. Sumanth, M.A., M.Phil., B.Ed., Head, Department of English, Erode Sengunthar Engineering College, Perundurai and I sincerely thank him.

I am thankful to Mr. M.Murali, M.Sc., for Statistical Analysis of the Data during the course of the research work. I also thank Mr. J. Raja and Ms. R. Amutha of Aryaas Computers who assisted me in the bringing the project in a good shape. I also thank the respondents of Erode district for sparing their valuable time in providing me the necessary data for this research work.

My special thanks to my beloved better-half (wife) Mrs. K.Shanthidevi B.A. (Corp), who gave moral, mental and physical strength to carry on this thesis and also I thank to my beloved Daughter Baby V. Mounisa, My friends and students for their blessings and constant encouragement.

I am thankful to Discovery Publishing House Pvt. Ltd., New Delhi, for their patience and diligence which has enabled me to present this book to the academic and practitioner communities.

Above all I am grateful to the Almighty for his blessings and grace.

T. VETRIVEL

Contents

List of Abbreviations

ACE	–	Acquired Customer Equity
CEM	–	Customer Efficiency Management
CIS	–	Customer Information System
CLV	–	Customer Lifetime Value
CRE	–	Customer Relationship Equity
CRM	–	Customer Relationship Management
CRS	–	Customer Relationship Share
CS/D	–	Customer Satisfaction/Dissatisfaction
CWER	–	Customers' Willingness to Engage in Relationship
FMCG	–	Fast Moving Consumer Goods
ICE	–	Integrated Customer Equity
KYC	–	Knowing Your Customer
MRP	–	Maximum Retail Price
NPD	–	New Product Development
RM	–	Relationship Marketing
SEM	–	Structural Equation Modelling
SERVQUAL	–	Services Quality
SFA	–	Sales Force Automation
SQ	–	Service Quality
STA	–	Sanpete Trade Association
VAT	–	Value Added Tax

Introduction and Design of the Study

INTRODUCTION

The most challenging aspect in a business is attracting the customers and retaining them throughout the period. A Customer Relationship Management (CRM) system offers a solution to this challenge by scientifically analyzing the dimensions of this challenge and by enabling the business organizations understand the complicated, multifaceted nature of its customers. Consequently, business organizations can evolve strategies based on the data of the above to attract the customers and retain them as well, by supplying them their wants and needs on analyzing the customers' business relationship with the business organization. This can make both the organization and the customers feel satisfied to their optimum level of satisfaction in their mutual business interaction. To sustain or survive and grow, business organizations find new ways of thinking which has led to new approaches, and has emerged in marketing research.

New technologies for distributing and collecting information have affected both companies and customers. Customers are continuously informed about products through different modes of communication. Sometimes they are drowning in too much information from different companies, but, on the whole the customer knowledge has no doubt been increased substantially. As knowledge increases, customers discover new options, thus the customer fidelity is decreased. However, with the new communicative media, companies can change their way of marketing as the possibility of gathering customer data is improved and thereby enhancing the scope of the business interactivity between the two has also become easier and rewarding. Further, the competition on the market is increasing domestically as well as globally. In order to achieve success, companies must find new long-term competitive advantages. It is not enough to rely on advanced technology in production and high quality product, because someone's competitors will soon have reached the same level. The solutions should be tailored after the customers' specific needs and wants, with the purpose to increase the customers' experienced value of the product or service. All these changes imply that there is an increasing need for new ways of thinking within this area.

The CRM highlights the importance of using Information Technology in creating, maintaining and enhancing customer relationships. However, it is not hassles free and there is a need to develop a better understanding of CRM and of how business concerns can use a CRM system to successfully ascend in business by wisely managing the data about the relationship between the customers and the business concern, largely depending upon the data pertaining to a particular business domain that could be effectively gathered.

Furthermore, this study will show that companies have a need for CRM functionality to support the Marketing, Sales, Order, Production, and Service Process. The CRM functionality can be divided into three main categories which are Marketing Automation, Sales Force Automation, and Customer Service and Support where each category comprises a number of different functional groups. The fact that companies are operating within the service or production industry doesn't seem to imply that the need for CRM functionality differs noticeably. However, there are several other aspects that seem to have an influence on the needs, such as the stage in the CRM development process, and the process-orientation of the organizations.

Consequently, by using customer information wisely to deliver what the customer needs, companies can create long-term, collaborative relationships with the customers. This will bring many advantages since long-term customers are less costly to serve and smooth-running relationships are less resource intensive. The CRM emerged for the reason that customers differ in their preferences and purchasing habits. Understandably, if the customers' needs and wishes were identical, there would be little use of CRM. Companies could continue to use mass marketing and mass communication without any risk of failure. Actually, customized marketing has been a reality for a long time, realized by niche firms positioning towards certain customers. However, it is only recently that mass customization of product and services has been a realistic objective. The enabling factor is that of IT.

The IT affects business activities in many different ways. Primarily, it can facilitate communication, information sharing and collaboration processes with customers and within a company or network. This is an important factor since it is independent of marketing approach; companies cannot operate effectively unless they have the capability to communicate rapidly, accurately and over a great distance and to mass of customers but almost with a personal reach out. The communication also needs to be two-way, integrated, recorded and managed.

Since the satisfaction of consumers' needs and wants is the justification for an organization's existence, an effective CRM system is a way for the organization to develop a customer focus in a business and it allows the organization to hear the customer's voice. Customer retention also means that the firm satisfies customers and/or offers variety as customer comes back and repeats transaction with the same organization. Customer retention and customer loyalty are the major benefits of CRM systems to the organization. Hence, an effective and successful CRM programme for a business organization requires creation of a customer-focused culture, effective adoption of customer-based measures, development of a complete end-to-end process to serve customers, suggestion of the questions to be asked to help a customer in solving the problem, recommendation of the strategies to deal with customer complaints, and tracking of all aspects of selling to both existing and prospective customers with a view to gain adequate customer support.

Even industrial leaders are now addressing how to transform their approach to customer management. Narrow functionally-based traditional marketing is being replaced by a new form of cross functional marketing by CRM. The traditional approach to marketing has been increasingly questioned in recent years. Formerly, marketing in business emphasized management of the key marketing mix elements only such as product, price, promotion and place within the functional context of the marketing domain or department. The adoption of CRM is based on the recent recognition that long-term relationships with customers are one of the most important assets of an organization and the information-enabled systems must be developed which will give them 'customer ownership'. Successful customer ownership will create competitive advantage and result in improved customer retention and profitability for the company.

It is also worth mentioning here that the performance of the sale of consumer goods was inconsistent in terms of sales in the recent past and there has recently been growth for over four years. Earlier the investors in this sector were not gainers at par with other booming sectors. After two years of such sinking performance of Fast Moving Consumer Goods sector, the year 2005 witnessed the demand for FMCGs (Fast Moving Consumer Goods) growing. Strong growth was seen across various segments in 2006. With the considerable rise in income liquidity in general and in India from 2006 and the good health enjoyed by the Indian economy, the urban consumers are continuing with their shopping spree. In such a juncture, this study is believed to have relevance and value to everyone concerned.

NEED FOR THE STUDY

In the Indian market, Customers are supposed to be treated as kings, following the business dictum given by the Father of nation Mahatma Gandhi, who pointed out that 'A shopkeeper should not think that he is doing any service to a customer, but he shall always remember that only the customer is doing a service to the shopkeeper by giving him an opportunity to do business with him'. As the nation prospers, and as the business expands with increasing competitiveness among the business players of a business domain this dictum gains more value since such customer-focus would not only fetch more profit but also would infuse some ethics and spirituality in business in the present cut-throat competitive scenario of business. Customer role is considered as the first requirement of business now. Therefore, every business concern is giving utmost importance to the customers' needs and wants, their immediate requirements, customers' perception on the products and its usage frequency. Due to increase in the level of education, exposure and the resultant expectations, most of the customers look for excellent quality in products and moderate price for them. They also seek the promotional offers like gift vouchers, extra contents added to the originally purchased item, price-off and attachment coupons, etc. as they believe the seller can afford to and the customers are worthy of it while they repeatedly shall have to do business with a seller.

The sellers are also aware of the fact that high quality service and customer satisfaction have been closely linked to profits, cost savings and market share. With this focus on the customer, leading companies are overhauling their traditional finance measurements of business performance and seeking new metrics (both internal and external) that include customers' perceptions and expectations.

The FMCG sellers normally do not and, in fact, cannot have a reliable customer data as they can do in other businesses like hotel industry, electronic goods suppliers/ sellers, car and automobile agencies and real estate dealers etc. since the data of the customers are obligatorily obtained for some reason or the other in such businesses. But the thoughtful FMCG retailers have started diplomatic means like some lucky draw on coupons on some crowded days/ occasions wherein the customers will have to fill in the details of the volume of purchase, contact number and address, purchase evidence, etc. though this data is not utilized properly for evolving any effective CRM system. Many of them either do not have any such data or know how to obtain any such data for the purpose of CRM, though all the retailers are selling the products with a focus on the customers' expectations. It is not known how far the customers' expectations are met by the retailers. To fill the void, this study is taken up, albeit in a smaller area, viz., Erode district as a descriptive endeavor.

STATEMENT OF THE PROBLEM

In today's world, the scope and use of Fast Moving Consumer Goods have expanded to such an extent that it is now claimed that this is considered to be the world's largest Industry with high rate of employee strength, and that which bring in a lot of revenue to the countries. On the other hand, the increased online price/product transparency and the new e-business modes (e.g. Online trading) enhance customers' purchasing decision, scope, powers, who are becoming more price sensitive, less brand loyal, more sophisticated and experience seekers.

The Consumer Products are experiencing increased globalization (from imported dates, soaps, stationery items to hair dyes, inclusive of imported chocolates and soft drinks), and hence global competition; on the other hand, this business requires the management of higher customer turnover, the challenge of convincing them within the shortest time they visit and transact their business, the growing customer acquisition costs and rising customer expectations. All this precisely means that the retailers' performance and competitiveness are significantly dependent on their ability to satisfy customers efficiently and effectively.

In the consumer retail business, the basic products such as perfumes, detergents, powders, shampoos, soaps, toothpastes, face creams, body sprays, hair oils, Food and health beverages, masala powders, branded flour, branded sugar, bakery products such as bread, biscuits, milk and dairy products, beverages such as tea, coffee, juices, bottled water, snack food, chocolates, etc., and other personal care products are produced and marketed by many and they are very similar. When a customer compares the quality levels that are identical he focuses on soft factors like personal treatment, personalization, one to one marketing and attention to the hospitality in the profession to get influenced by the seller as well as to repeatedly visit the same seller.

But for an effective CRM, an exhaustive customer data base is mandatory. In order to compete on a highly competitive market a retailer has to meet every single customer's needs and expectations and should have a record of the same to refer back, develop and interact with. To do this, it is important to understand the aspects of business performance that persuade customers to become repeat purchasers, and to exhibit behavioural loyalty.

To enhance profitability and customers' satisfaction, retailers must now-a-days focus on implementing Customer Relationship Management (CRM) strategies that aim to seek, gather and store right information, validate and share it throughout the entire organization that could offer solutions and be a pointer to extend the necessary attention to individual customers in order to attract and retain them. As far as retailers of Fast Moving Consumer Goods (FMCG) are concerned, there is no CRM practice except for a very meagre CRM interaction with the customers through some traditional, unscientific, not-so productive and arbitrary factors like prime location of the shop, huge investment for gorgeous attraction for the shop and targeting only the elite customers. Xu states that:

> "Basically, CRM is an idea regarding how a company can keep their most profitable customers by increasing the value of interaction. The value is maximized through differentiation of the management of customer relationships".

Fast Moving Consumer Goods is a perfect area for the appliance of CRM principles and maximizing the profit. Customer Relationship Management is a business strategy by selecting and managing the Customer Relationship through simplest means like sending SMS via cell phones that would enable one-to-one marketing plans (by offering personalized services). Giving value-added services and making the customer satisfied to win loyalty and retention from the customer also could be a best strategy for retail stores to differentiate themselves from their competitors. Customer Relationship Management implementation, particularly in retail store services, is very challenging. In retail stores a successful CRM strategy cannot be implemented by only installing and integrating software packages, it needs to be coordinated with the other business operations, business strategy and in getting the user and customer acceptance for the same.

Erode District, which is a business and industrial area where the per capita income is high (famous for oil industry, cotton & textile industry, turmeric industry, sugar industry, some Fast Moving Consumer Products and manipulations of agricultural products) and it contributes considerably to the revenue of the state income, Rs. 3296.09 crores. This is one of the main trading centres in India. Hence, the FMCG products are having fast movement in all the areas in this district. Therefore, retailers have started having increased avenues for selling, like Mega-shopping Malls, Departmental stores, etc. In the current situation, most of the retailers of FMCG fill the needs and wants of the customers. And they seriously view customers' perception and opinion, satisfactory level of customers and the problems faced by them in doing business while the customers find difficulties in selecting the products in their selected retail stores and in obtaining satisfactory services from the retailers. These are the major issues faced by the retailers with customers.

Based on the above issues the following questions are probed in the present study:

1. To what extent do the FMCG retailers concentrate in establishing a good CRM practice in Erode district?
2. What are the factors that influence the customers for repeated purchase and retention of the same retail store?
3. What are the common problems faced by both retailers and customers?

OBJECTIVES OF THE STUDY

1. To study the retailing industry in general and in particular FMCG retailers of Erode District.
2. To evaluate the customers' opinion and expectations in FMCG retail business.

3. To identify the level of satisfaction perceived by the customers on CRM practiced by the retailers in the study area.
4. To study the retailers' perception in retailing of Fast Moving Consumer Goods.
5. To describe the retailers' style of building relationship with customers.
6. To explain and evaluate the implementation of customer services and its relationship with CRM.
7. To identify the problems faced by both retailers and customers of FMCG.
8. To suggest better ways and means for developing good customer relationship.

METHODOLOGY

The validity of any research depends on the systematic method of collecting the data, and analyzing the same in appropriate order. In the present study, both primary and secondary data were collected. In this study, descriptive research was used.

DESCRIPTIVE RESEARCH DESIGN

Descriptive research design is a scientific method which involves observing and describing the behaviour of a subject without influencing it in any way. Many scientific disciplines, especially social science and psychology, use this method to obtain a general overview of the subject.

Descriptive research is also called Statistical Research. The main goal of this type of research is to describe the data and characteristics about what is being studied. The idea behind this type of research is to study frequencies, averages, and other statistical calculations. Although this research is highly accurate, it does not gather the causes behind a situation. Descriptive research is mainly done when a researcher wants to gain a better understanding of a topic for example, a frozen ready meals company learns that there is a growing demand for fresh ready meals but doesn't know much about the area of fresh food and so has to carry out research in order to gain a better understanding. It is quantitative and uses surveys and panels and also the use of probability sampling.

Descriptive research is the exploration of the existing certain phenomena. The details of the facts won't be known. The existing phenomena facts are not known to the persons. This research seeks to depict what already exists in a group or population. Descriptive studies do not seek to measure the effect of a variable; they seek only to describe. Descriptive research answers the questions who, what, where, when and how. In this work, descriptive research was used to describe the demographic characteristics of both retailers and customers. In short descriptive research deals with everything that can be counted and studied.

SAMPLE DESIGN

Sampling is the use of a subset of the population to represent the whole population. Probability sampling, or random sampling, is a sampling technique in which the probability of getting any particular sample may be calculated. Non-probability sampling does not meet this criterion and should be used with caution. Non-probability sampling techniques cannot be used to infer from the sample to the general population. Any generalizations obtained from a non-probability sample must be filtered through one's knowledge of the topic being studied. Performing non-probability sampling is considerably less expensive than doing probability sampling, but the results are of limited value.

For collecting primary data, field survey technique was employed in the study. First-hand information was collected from 510 retailers and 1140 customers of Erode district. The respondents were chosen from the entire Erode district, based on the members listed in the Retailers Association in

Erode District. The respondents were selected through Probability method of Random Sampling technique for Retailers' survey and non-probability convenience sampling technique was adopted for collecting data from the Customers.

DATA COLLECTION

Primary Data

The primary data were collected from the Retailers and the Customers whoever were selling and buying FMCG in Erode District. The information was gathered through personal interview method. In order to fulfil the objectives set, a sample study was undertaken by using a well-framed questionnaire that was duly filled in by the respondents. Respondents with varying background were selected based on the important aspects of their gender, age, educational qualifications, occupation, income, etc. They are all situated throughout the Erode district. The specimen of the questionnaire given to the selected sample respondents is shown in the Appendix of this thesis.

Secondary Data

The primary data were supplemented by a spate of secondary sources of data. The secondary data were gathered from the records of FMCG retailers Association and Erode Collectrate. Latest information in the FMCG sector was gathered from well-equipped libraries of Bangalore, Coimbatore and Chennai. Internet web resources were also used. Also the secondary data were collected from leading journals such as *The Indian Journal of Marketing, Journal of Indian Management, Customer Relationship Management Practices and Economic Survey Report.*

TOOLS OF DATA COLLECTION

By virtue of mass data obtained from the research survey as well as the data collected from secondary sources, descriptive and analytical research were considered the most appropriate for the study. The research problems and the questionnaire were all framed accordingly. The suggestions offered in the final chapter of the present research report emerged from the inferences drawn from the study of the sample respondents (the retailers and customers of Erode dist.). The researcher used both close-ended and open-ended questions in the questionnaire to collect the necessary primary data.

PILOT STUDY

The questionnaire meant for the respondents was pre-tested with 40 respondents of each category (the retailers and the customers who purchased FMCG products). After pre-testing, necessary modifications were made in the questionnaire on getting the advice from subject experts and the research supervisor to fit in the same on the track of the present study.

FRAMEWORK OF ANALYSIS

The core of the study being 'Customer Relationship Management', the study centres on the dependent variable viz., level of satisfaction perceived by the customers, retailers perception, problems relating to customer relationship management and the relationship of the same with the related independent variables.

APPROACH TO THE ESTABLISHMENT OF RAPPORT WITH CUSTOMERS

The difference in the extent of service among the FMCG retailers is based on their year of establishment, experience in retailing business, number of retail outlets owned and mode of purchase and mode of deliverance to customers. These factors were studied through Two-Way tables, Percentage analysis, Averages, Weighted Average Analysis, Ranges and Standard Deviation. Further, ANOVA, Chi-square Test, Multiple Regression Analysis, Multi-discriminant Analysis and Factor Analysis were used for this research study. In addition, ranking positions of the specified problems were found using Henry Garrett Ranking Method was employed.

ANOVA

The degree of influence of the independent variables pertaining to retailers is listed as follows:

1. Year of establishment
2. Experience in retail business
3. Number of outlets owned
4. Mode of purchase of FMCG products

CHI-SQUARE TEST

The degree of influence of the independent variables was made by analyzing the customers' relationship with the selected FMCG retailer respondents. The following independent variables were tested with the help of Chi-square χ^2 test. They are:

(i) Respondents' age
(ii) Respondents' gender
(iii) Respondents' educational qualifications
(iv) Respondents' occupation
(v) Respondents' monthly Income
(vi) Respondents' marital Status
(vii) Respondents' family size
(viii) Level of awareness
(ix) Period of relationship with the shop
(x) Preference of the retailer over others

In order to identify the factors influencing the customers' rapport among the retailers, a Chi-square (χ^2) test was used and the formula applied is given below:

$$\chi^2 = \sum \frac{(O - E)^2}{E}$$

with Degree of Freedom (D.F.) = (c–1) (r–1)

Where,

O = Observed frequency,

E = Expected frequency,

c = Number of Columns,

r = Number of Rows.

MULTIPLE REGRESSION ANALYSIS

The regression is a statistical relationship between two or more variables. When there are two or more independent variables, the analysis that describes such relationship is the Multiple Regression. This analysis is adopted where there is one dependent variable that is presumed to be a functionary of two or more independent variables. In Multiple Regression, a linear composite of explanatory variables is formed in such a way that it has the maximum correlation with an active criterion variable. The main objective of using this technique is to predict the variability of the dependent variable, based on its co-variance with all the independent variables. It is useful to predict the level of dependent phenomenon through Multiple Regression Analysis Models, if the levels of independent variables were given. The Linear Multiple Regression Problem is to estimate coefficients b_1, b_2, . . ., b_j and b_0 such that the expression

$$Y = \beta_0 + \beta_1 X_1 + \beta_2 X_2 + . . . + \beta_j X_K$$

provides a good estimate of an individual Y score based on the X scores, where

Y = Level of Satisfaction

X_1 = Age

X_2 = Gender

X_3 = Educational Qualifications

X_4 = Occupation

X_5 = Monthly Income

X_6 = Marital Status

X_7 = Family size

X_8 = Level of Awareness

X_9 = Period of relationship with the shop

X_{10} = Preference of the retailer over others and

$\beta_0 + \beta_1 + \beta_2 + \ldots + \beta_j$ are the parameters to be estimated.

HENRY GARRETT RANKING TECHNIQUE

This technique was used to rank the reasons and problems faced by the customers and type of customers, customers preferences and expected products opined by the retailers. In this method the respondents were asked to rank the reasons and problems. The order of merit given by the respondents was converted into ranks by using the following formula.

$$\text{Percentage Position} = \frac{100\left(R_{ij} - 0.5\right)}{N_j}$$

The percentage position of each rank thus obtained is converted into scores by referring to the table given by Henry Garrett. Then for each factor the scores of individual respondents were added and divided by the total number of respondents for whom the scores were added. These mean scores for all the factors were arranged in the order of their ranks and inferences were drawn.

WEIGHTED AVERAGE METHOD

The weighted average is similar to a simple percentage, where instead of each of the data points contribute equally to the final average, some data points contribute more than others. The notion of weighted average plays an important role in descriptive statistics.

Formally, the weighted mean of a non-empty set of data

$[x_1, x_2, \ldots, x_n]$,

With non-negative weights

$[w_1, w_2, \ldots, w_n]$,

is the quantity calculated by

$$\bar{x} = \sum_{i=1}^{n} w_i x_i / \sum_{i=l}^{n} w_i$$

This means,

$$\bar{x} = \frac{w_1 x_1 + w_2 x_2 + \ldots w_n x_n}{w_1 + w_2 + \ldots + w_n}$$

The data elements with a high weight contribute more to the weighted mean than the elements with a low weight. The weights must not be negative.

In this analysis the retailers' opinion on customers behaviour, customers queries, their relationship and customers awareness about the Fast Moving Consumer Goods and depth of parameters can be given weightages and compound scoring can be estimated. The strong or highest opinion in the acceptance area will be given the maximum weightages and the non-acceptance area will be given lower weightages. And also the customers opinion like

Product mix, Promotion mix, Price mix and Place mix strategies were measured using weighted average method.

HYPOTHESES

1. Implementation of CRM model will increase FMCG customers' satisfaction, loyalty, and retention.
2. Customers' Income and Educational Qualifications will help them to select the products in the market.
3. Personalization of services according to customers' preferences and characteristics will increase their satisfaction.
4. A good customer support and services will increase customer satisfaction and loyalty.

SCOPE OF THE STUDY

In order to describe how companies can use a CRM system, this research gives a description of how CRM functionality can be used at different steps in the sales process. Certain functionality is generally applicable and can be used at many different steps in the sales process, while some functions can be connected to a specific step. The analysis will show that the functionality included in the main functional categories is used in all phases in the sales process. For example, Customer Service and Support functionality is not only needed for service activities, the results from measuring customer satisfaction can also be useful when deciding who to target in a campaign. Consequently, the connection between CRM functionality and the sales process will give a complete view on how a CRM system can be used. And also the study will help the FMCG retailers in formulating and enforcing CRM strategies in this sector.

PERIOD OF THE STUDY

The research was conducted for a period of three and half years. The period of the study was confined to 2006 to

2009. The first year was spent on collecting the review of literature, and the second year was spent on collecting the opinion from the retailers and customers. Data analysis and interpretation, correction and finalizing the thesis were done during the rest of the period.

LIMITATIONS OF THE STUDY

The study takes into account the following limitations:

1. Market survey was conducted only in the Erode District of Tamilnadu. Further, the survey method which was adopted for collecting the data in this study has its own limitations.
2. Only 510 retailers and 1140 customers were selected for eliciting first-hand information. In view of the time and monetary constraints involved, it was not possible to contact more than the selected number of respondents.
3. Certain respondents gave information about their economic backgrounds from their memory as they had no recorded account of them or else were hesitant of revealing. Hence, the generalization of the findings of the study is subject to limitations.

CHAPTER SCHEME

The present empirical study has been divided into Seven Chapters.

- ❖ The *First Chapter* gives the extensive but clear picture of research design, which includes Introduction to CRM, Need for the Study in the retail business domain and in the study area Erode, Statement of the Problem, Objectives of the Study, Hypotheses and Scope of the Study, Period covered by the Study, Limitations of the Study, Research Methodology adopted, and Frame Work of Analysis.
- ❖ The *Second Chapter* discusses the previous studies relevant to the present research.

- The *Third Chapter* focuses on the conceptual framework of customer relationship management.
- The *Fourth Chapter* highlights an overview of the marketing of FMCG products and the progress of FMCG retailers of Erode district.
- The *Fifth Chapter* covers the ways and means of the FMCG retailers' practicing of CRM and the problems faced by them in the study area.
- The *Sixth Chapter* presents the FMCG customers' opinion on CRM practices by the FMCG sector of Erode.
- The *Seventh Chapter* recapitulates the key Findings and Conclusions of the study. At the end of this chapter, certain Suggestions have been put forth for better Customer Relationship Management by the FMCG retailers of Erode district.

Review of Literature

> There is only one boss, the Customer. He can fire everybody in the company, from the Chairman down, simply by spending his money somewhere else"
>
> – Sam Walton- founder Wal-Mart Stores.

INTRODUCTION

Continuous changes in the economic scenario and intense competition are causing businesses of today to undergo radical changes in the approach to business. A number of new technologies are being incorporated in the infrastructure to create a more profitable status. Unlike before, today everything begins and ends with the Customer as the emerging global and electronic economy has turned on its head, and has placed the customers firmly in the controlling seat.

EVOLUTION OF CRM

Developing Customer Relationships has historical antecedents going back to the pre-industrialization era. In the pre-industrialization era developing direct customer relationship was the only means to carry on business transaction. This was due to the fact that economy was the only means to carry out business transaction. 1960s was the era of mass marketing, in 1970s the focus was on segment marketing, in 1980s transaction marketing became niche competitive advantage and in 1990s relationship marketing came into vogue.

The CRM (Customer Relationship Management) – Management *mantra* of the new millennium has gained predominance in today's market and AMR research Inc. predicts that the customer relationship management market will reach $16.8 billion by the year 2010, and a compound annual growth rate of 49 per cent over the next five years.

Parasuraman et al. (1985)[1] in their study entitled "A Conceptual Model of Service Quality and its Implications for Future Research" highlighted that the attainment of quality in products and services has become a pivotal concern of the 1980s. While quality in tangible goods has been described and measured by marketers, quality in services is largely undefined and unresearched. The authors attempt to rectify this situation by reporting the insights obtained in an extensive exploratory investigation of quality in four service businesses and by developing a model of service quality. Propositions and recommendations to stimulate future research about service quality are offered.

GROWTH OF FMCG

McDermott *et al.* (1997)[2] in their study entitled "The Distribution of Fast-Moving Consumer Goods in the People's Republic of China" highlighted that the article looks at the distribution of fast-moving consumer goods (FMCG) and the consumer market in China. As a developing country, China (as well as underdeveloped countries) is associated with inefficient marketing and distribution of products. The traditional distribution system of China was known as a "fenpei" or allocation system. China's retail trade was also dominated by state owned stores which were supplemented on a limited scale by small private and individual retail operators. China's Ministry of Commerce managed and controlled distribution channels for all types of consumer products. The authors note that since China's department stores have enjoyed greater autonomy in matters of merchandising, more domestic and foreign funded factories are selling directly to them.

Bolton, Ruth Lemon and Katherine (1999)[3] in their study entitled "A Dynamic Model of Customers' Usage of Services: Usage as an Antecedent and Consequence of Satisfaction" highlight that as firms seek ways to manage customer relationships over the long term, understanding the dynamics of the service provider-customer relationship becomes a key priority. In this article, the authors develop and test a dynamic model of customer usage of services, identifying causal links between customer's prior usage levels, satisfaction evaluations, and subsequent service usage. The authors quantify the (heretofore anecdotal) relationship between customer satisfaction and subsequent service usage and provide new theoretical insights into the antecedents of customer satisfaction by introducing the concept of perceived payment equity. The primary contribution of the article is an understanding of how service usage changes over time, and particularly, how the consumer's view of the fairness or 'equity' of the exchange over time affects the consumer's usage of services. By examining the antecedents of payment equity, it can be determined how customers use price and usage over time to update their evaluations of the fairness of the exchange. This evaluation affects overall satisfaction, which in turn affects future usage. The results suggest that customers' usage levels can be managed through pricing strategies, communications, and more generally dynamic customer satisfaction management.

Castelo, Pita and Jose (2000)[4], in their study entitled "An Empirical Examination of the Antecedents of Customer Loyalty in Retail Banking in Spain" highlight that

Customer loyalty, Customer Satisfaction/Dissatisfaction (CS/D) and Service Quality (SQ) are some of the most substantial concepts in marketing. Although there has been extensive research relating to these concepts, this has been irregularly discussed. Thus, CS/D research to date has almost entirely concentrated on products, fundamentally low-involvement, non durable, while almost no attention has been paid to services in general, nor to financial services and retail banking, in particular. As for Service Quality research, this has been more concentrated on services rather than on goods, although this model has been criticized recently by various researchers. Customer loyalty is an underlying objective for marketing, and the causal relationship between customer loyalty and profits has been widely recognized.

The main objective of this research is an empirical test, for the first time, of the relationship between CS/D and SQ, and the impact of a new variable (usage rate) on customer loyalty in the context of retail banking. The data used to test the path model were collected from a cross-sectional survey of 384 retail banking customers from north-western Spain. The only variable found to have a direct impact upon customer loyalty was disconfirmation. When both direct and indirect effects are accounted for, performance also impacts on customer loyalty through disconfirmation, while usage rate does not seem to have any effect. Finally, an analysis of the performance, usage rate, and loyalty items reveals dimensions substantially different from previous studies.

These findings considerably help towards an understanding of the complex process of customer loyalty determination for services, and retail banking in particular. They also have significant implications for bank managers.

CUSTOMER LOYALTY

Zahay and Debra L (2000)[5] in their study entitled "Aligning Strategy and Customer Information for

Performance in Business Markets" highlight that the major goals of this research are to determine how to measure how well business units manage Customer Information and place these capabilities in the context of their strategic choices of positioning and segmentation. This research supports the theoretical concept that learning organisation theory provides an organizing framework for operationalizing the measures of how well business units manage Customer Information and a way to measure these capabilities.

The relationship between the Customer Information System (CIS) and Marketing Performance in terms of share of wallet, customer retention, lifetime customer value and return on investment is supported by this research, although somewhat overshadowed by the effect of strategic positioning choice. Marketing Performance variables mediate positioning strategy; the CIS and the ultimate performance variable increases in business unit sales and net income. The true value of the CIS in the organisation might be the ability to manage through these important matrices.

Although there is support for the idea that strategy and information management should be aligned to achieve competitive advantage, just implementing an effective strategy combination helps the business unit achieve competitive advantage as measured by the Marketing Performance variables above and by business unit growth. The decision to follow the "Both" strategy (Low-Cost and Differentiation simultaneously) could be considered a surrogate for "Strategic Excellence" in general. This strategy is associated with competitive advantage (Treacy and Wieserma 1993) and in most cases requires coordination of information throughout the business unit as well as a deep and sophisticated knowledge of the customer.

Zakheim, Betty (2000)[6] in his study entitled "CRM's Risky Relationship with Telecom" highlight that in telecom, acquiring and retaining customers is a particularly tall order. The Web provides great opportunity to distinguish a carrier and its online retail channels by providing convenience and 24/7 support. Event-triggered e-mails are an effective vehicle for increasing customer satisfaction, and can even help prevent churn. The Web also provides another touch point to get to know customers better and cater to their preferences.

Foss and Stone (2001)[7] in their study entitled "Customer Relationship Management and Loyalty Schemes" highlight that relationship marketing shifts the focus of the marketing exchange from transactions to relationships Relationship marketing acknowledges that a stable customer base is a core business asset. The essence and nature of relationships and their business value are encapsulated in the concept of customer loyalty, and its associated literature. The benefit of customer loyalty is a provider of either service or relationship.

CUSTOMER SERVICE QUALITY MODEL

Hagy and Richard Alan(2001)[8] in their study titled "An Empirical Examination of Customer Perceptions of Service Quality Utilizing the Extended Service Quality Model under the Condition of Multiple Subunit Service Providers" revealed that the dominant conceptualization of service quality in the service management literature has been the specification of service quality as the gap between the customer's expectations for service (what a customer feels a service firm should offer) versus the customer's perception of the service performance that was delivered by a firm. This gap between expectations and perceptions is often referred to as the disconfirmation construct of service quality, and is frequently measured by the 22-item SERVQUAL instrument developed by Parasuraman, *et.al.* (1985). This study explored the reliability and validity of the SERVQUAL scale for the measurement of student perceptions of service quality of a university housing programme in a nonprofit higher education firm. Gap 1 of the Extended Service Quality Model, defined as the discrepancy between customer expectations and management's perceptions of customer expectations, was also examined along with its theorized contributing factors (marketing research orientation, upward communication, and levels of management) across five subunit organisations involved in the production of the housing programme. The study provided support for the psychometric performance of the SERVQUAL instrument in a non-profit higher education firm; reported significant differences in student perceptions of service quality according to gender and grade classification where females, sophomores and seniors perceived lower service quality; and, found that a significant Gap 1 existed between managers and customers. Moderate relationships were found between service quality, subunit satisfaction, overall satisfaction, value, and a willingness to recommend the programme. Lastly, a structural model with the causal ordering of service quality and value as antecedent to satisfaction provided a good fit to the data and accounted for 64 per cent of the variance in a student's willingness to recommend the housing programme to a friend.

Atkin, Thomas S (2001)[9] in his study entitled "The Impact of Negotiation Strategy on Customer-supplier Relationships" explained that the research sets forth an investigation of the negotiation process and its impact on the relationships between organisations. In particular, it seeks to examine the effects that negotiation strategies such as coercion and contract formality have upon outcomes such as satisfaction. A model of negotiation behaviour is offered to better explain and predict the negotiation process as it contributes to the establishment of relationships between organisations.

The hypothesized model is also tested across a variety of relationship categories that exist between suppliers and customers. Data were collected by surveying undergraduate students at a large mid-western university while they participated in a negotiation simulation. A total of 264 cases were used in the analysis.

Following preliminary data analysis, regression and Structural Equation Modeling (SEM) were used to assess construct validity and test the model's hypotheses. Results demonstrated that there is a significant negative effect of coercive negotiation strategy on satisfaction. The results also show that the magnitude of this effect can vary according to the type of relationship the parties have developed.

Verhoef *et. al.* (2001)[10] in their study entitles "The Impact of Satisfaction and Payment Equity on Cross-buying: A Dynamic model for a Multi-service Provider" concluded that's the last decade, marketers have primarily focused on keeping customers. Only recently have they become aware that creating value by cross-selling additional services is also an important aspect of customer relationship management. In this article they investigate how satisfaction and payment equity, defined as the perceived fairness of the price, affect cross-buying at a multi-service provider. They also consider its competitors' performance on these factors. Their results show that the effect of satisfaction differs between customers with lengthy and short relationships. It also shows that payment equity negatively affects cross-buying for customers with long relationships. However, if the prices of the supplier are fairer than the prices of the competitor, then the customers' probability of cross-buying will increase.

Garden (2001)[11] in his study entitled "Retailers say CRM is Crucial but few are Implementing Initiatives Anonymous" suggest that Retailers consider CRM initiatives crucial to the success of their business, but few retailers are implementing CRM strategies, a new Gartner, Inc. (www.gartner.com) survey reports. Fifty-two per cent of respondents rated CRM as their highest business priority, 43 per cent rated CRM as a moderate business priority, and 5 per cent rated it as a low priority. But on the whole, only 34 per cent of respondents acknowledged deploying a CRM initiative.

Yu, Larry (2001)[12] in his study entitled "Successful Customer-Relationship Management" highlighted that being close to the customer is the key to success in the marketplace. That mantra of modern marketing has led to a boom in information-technology spending to help companies get in touch with their customers. Indeed, interest in customer relationship management (CRM) systems continues to heat up. The key is for the CRM effort to move beyond sales, marketing, customer services and assisting customers to include operations and the "Office of the CEO" or strategic planning.

Feinberg *et. al.* (2002)[13] in their study entitled "The State of Electronic Customer Relationship Management in Retailing" comments on the availability of Electronic Customer Relationship Management (E-CRM) features on retail Web sites and their relationship to consumer satisfaction and site traffic. The top 100 specialty stores, standard retail stores, and Internet retailer Web sites were analyzed for the presence of 41 E-CRM features. The availability of these features was then assessed for their relationship with consumer traffic to the site and customer satisfaction with the site. Internet retailers were significantly more likely to have E-CRM attributes on their site. However, only the chat feature, spare parts availability, gift certificate purchase, mailing address, search engine, links, and a company profile were associated with customer satisfaction. No E-CRM feature was associated with customer traffic to a site. Standard retailers appear to be behind in implementing E-CRM features in current operations. It is not clear that retailers understand what aspects of E-CRM will be important in customer satisfaction.

Xue, Mei (2002)[14] in his study entitled "Customer efficiency: Concept and its Impact on Service Management" investigated the impact of the increasing participation of customers in service delivery processes that has been enabled by the advances in information technology. The concept of Customer Efficiency (CE) is introduced along with a conceptual framework for Customer Efficiency Management (CEM) described in the study, a game-theoretic model is developed in order to study competition among service providers when self-service is an option. The analysis of the equilibrium from this model shows that, given average customer efficiency, the proportion of the service task outsourced to the customer is a decisive factor in the resulting competitive equilibrium. These results show that self-service through the Internet has a significant migration effect on personal service and, consequently, saves service delivery costs and improves customer efficiency.

CONSUMERS' PERCEPTIONS AND ATTITUDES:

Wayment, Tawna (2002)[15] in their study entitled "Analyses of Consumers' Perceptions and Attitudes Towards Services and Products offered by a Craft Cooperative in Rural Utah" highlighted that the purpose of the study was to develop a profile of the Sanpete Trade Association's (STA) typical consumer, to examine the attitudes and perceptions consumers had towards the products and service quality at STA, and to determine if service quality impacted consumers' purchasing behaviour.

The study indicated that a consumer's attitude towards the products and his or her perception of service quality offered could be used to predict whether a consumer spent money at the STA. Customer's age along with consumers who were first time visitors, also significantly predicted purchasing behaviour, it was also noted that trends existed between purchasing behaviour and the factors of age, education, marital status, and income. The results will provide direction for incorporating service quality into business management strategies.

Li Kam Wa and Peter (2002)[16] in their study entitled "The Critical Success Factors of Customer Relationship Management (CRM) technological initiatives" highlighted that customers are any organisations' best assets. As an increasing number of organisations realize the importance of becoming more customer-centric in today's competitive economy, they are also discovering that they must deliver knowledge about their customers, products, and services internally (i.e across multiple organisational functions) and externally (i.e at all customer touch points). Therefore, enterprise executives are interested in knowing the Critical Success Factors that will drive their Customer Relationship Management (CRM) technological initiatives. CRM technological initiatives help foster a customer-centric business strategy, the diffusion of knowledge, a unified face to all customers, and a holistic view of customers.

The core finding of this study reveals that technological readiness alone does not lead to successful CRM technological initiatives. Possessing knowledge management capabilities emerges as the most significant critical success factor of CRM technological initiatives and is strongly related to technological readiness. Top management support is significant for all CRM technological initiatives with the exception of the SFA (Sales Force Automation) of CRM Infrastructure.

CUSTOMERS, BELIEF AND EXPERIENCE

Severt, Denver Eugene (2002)[17] in his study entitled "The Customer's Path to Loyalty: A Partial Test of the Relationships of Prior Experience, Justice, and Customer Satisfaction" explain that the service sector is the fastest growing segment of the economy, responsible for 75 per cent of the GNP, and still growing. Its success is important to the global economy. Nonetheless, throughout the 20-year evolution of services marketing literature, research that guides theory, methodology, and practice for service success has remained underrepresented. Published research regarding the effect of customers' justice perceptions on customer satisfaction is primarily experimental and focuses only on service recovery after a service failure, providing insufficient information about how the justice experienced in a service encounter affects a customer's satisfaction level. Proactive and reactive service recovery research abounds; service failures have overshadowed service success.

This is the first empirical research to investigate across service outcomes the effects (1) of interactional, distributive, and procedural justice on overall justice and customer satisfaction and (2) of overall justice on customer satisfaction. A cross-sectional written survey was used to gather data relevant to the eight hypotheses proposed and shown on the measurement model. Sixty per cent of the 302 respondents recalled satisfying service encounters and 40 per cent recalled dissatisfying service encounters. This research provides practical information that can lead to a better understanding of customers' evaluation methods and be used to guide the formation of improved service strategies that provide justice, a key to satisfaction.

Cho, Yooncheong (2002)[18] in his study entitled "The Effects of Post-purchase Evaluation Factors on Online vs. In-store Customer Complaining Behaviour" explained how businesses handle a customer's complaining behaviour has been referred to as the critical "moment of truth" (Tax, *et. al.* 1998) in managing and developing E-Commerce Customer Relationship Management (eCCRM). This study contends that understanding customer complaining behaviour and handling customer complaints provides implications for e-business about what managerial changes should be made for effective complaint management and also for successful e-commerce customer relationship management. The purpose of this study is to investigate the effects of post-purchase evaluation factors on customers' propensity to complain in the online versus in-store shopping environments. In particular, this study examines how the online environment differs from the in-store environment, in terms of the relative importance of various factors on customer complaining behaviour. Post-purchase evaluation factors, such as the degree of dissatisfaction, importance of the purchase, perceived benefits and costs from complaining, personal characteristics, situational influences, propensity to complain, and customer loyalty have been developed in the online context and applied in this study. More sophisticated analysis is performed by examining the effects of the post-purchase evaluation factors on propensity to complain by the product classification on the Web.

This study contributes to effective complaint management, particularly for e-businesses, suggesting that certain managerial changes, such as increased service quality could result in different and more desirable behaviours, perhaps profoundly affecting customer loyalty myopia. Such myopia stems from believing that e-loyalty can be created and sustained in and by it without regard to how complaints are handled.

Treytl, Kristina Joy (2002[19]) in his study entitled "The Impact of Employee Satisfaction on Customer Satisfaction with the Sales Interaction" stressed on the link between employee satisfaction and customer satisfaction in an attempt to drive customer satisfaction and profitability. However, little research has been conducted focusing on the satisfaction of specific employee groups on a particular facet of customer satisfaction. This study examined the relationship between the satisfaction of sales professionals and the overall satisfaction customers reported with the sales process. Employee satisfaction data of sales professionals from a Fortune 500 software company were correlated with data from the customer satisfaction survey. The results indicated a significant correlation between employee satisfaction with training, management, performance management and compensation/benefits. Business implications of these results are discussed.

Paul Krill (2002)[20] in his study entitled "The CRM of the Crop" threw lighten CRM's status as an application deployment nightmare; two technology heavyweights have revealed their CRM strategies in a move that highlight divergent views on the role of Web services. Both Microsoft and AT&T agree that implementing an internal CRM strategy is no picnic but a point of departure has emerged over how large enterprises can simplify the complexity of enterprise integration. Executives from the companies used separate presentations at Frost & Sullivan's recent CRM conference to detail the challenges of their experience with CRM, reflecting widespread concerns about the successful implementation of the technology.

Payant and W. Randall (2003)[21] in their study entitled 'The Challenges and Opportunities of Customer Profitability Analysis' pointed out the shortcomings of customer relationship management (CRM) technology in the U.S.A. Recent survey by a non-profit trade association revealed that nearly half of the banks responding were not satisfied with the information being provided by their customer profitability measurement processes. Similarly, other surveys reveal many bank executives are equally dissatisfied with the returns received on their large investment in technology. The first well-documented shortcoming is that many CRM systems primarily focus on technologizing the sales process. The second shortcoming is that many CRM profitability measures rest on traditional cost accounting approaches typically found in manufacturing, wholesaling and retailing environments.

CUSTOMERS' RETENTION

Wu, Wei (2003)[22] in their study entitled "Customer Relationship Management (CRM) Technology, Market Orientation, and Organisational Performance" discussed the relationship among Customer Relationship Management (CRM) technology, organisational market orientation, perceived customer retention improvement, and perceived performance improvement from using CRM technology. The data collected by mail survey from eighty Canadian organisations were analyzed to understand how organisations achieve benefits from investment in CRM technology. The findings suggest that first, the CRM technology, used to enhance organisational capability of serving customer, is positively linked to perceived customer retention improvement and perceived performance improvement; second, companies with higher level of market orientation are more likely to adopt CRM technology; third, there is a positive link between organisational market orientation and perceived customer retention improvement and perceived performance improvement. This study contributes to the MIS discipline by demonstrating the enabling role and business value of information technology in customer relationship management, as well as by underscoring market orientation, the organisational resource that can possibly increase the effect of CRM technology on customer retention and overall performance.

DeFazio Vincent James (2003)[23] in his study entitled "Customer Service Leadership Skills and Customer Relationship Management" highlighted that the quantitative descriptive research correlates the influence of a set of leadership skills and customer relationship capabilities of customer service representatives with the operational management of customer relationships in an Internet Service Provider organisation. The intent of this research was to address the problem of ineffective organisational leadership in using customer relationship management (CRM) skills and capabilities of sales and service personnel in achieving the level of customer relationships required to sustain successful business. Industry wise, up to 70 per cent of the CRM initiatives fail and 57 per cent cannot justify the investment in CRM programmes that use traditional approaches. The results of this research study indicated that an investment in customer service representative leadership skills contributed to emotional, cognitive, and customer relationship capabilities. The investment in CSR leadership skills can yield significant improvement in customer satisfaction at a fraction of the cost of traditional CRM investments. A unique mix of leadership skills and CRM capabilities will enhance customer relationships and will constitute a competitive advantage that translates into customer retention, more up-sell and cross-sell opportunities, and an increased life-time value of customers.

Saini, Amit (2003)[24] in his study entitled "Organisational Assimilation of Technology for Relationship Marketing: The Case of Customer Relationship Management (CRM)" suggested that Customer Relationship Management (CRM), an integration of information technology and business processes, allows marketers to execute relationship marketing at an enterprise-wide level. This dissertation examines the notion of CRM assimilation in the context of marketing organisations. CRM assimilation is defined as the acceptance, utilization and know-how of an IT based CRM system in planning and implementing a firm's relationship marketing strategies and activities. Finally, it was also established that CRM assimilation positively impacted CRM Performance.

Singh, Siddharth Shekhar (2003)[25] in his study entitled "Customer Lifetime Value Analysis" found that the firms were increasingly adopting a customer-centric approach to marketing, and in this context, Customer Lifetime Value (CLV) became critical. This dissertation investigated some important issues arising in CLV analysis. It is divided into three main parts with each investigating specific issues.

The first part develops a continuous time Markov chain-based framework that allows a more general method for estimating the total value of a firm's present and future customers (Integrated Customer Equity (ICE)). The framework is applied to link marketing actions to customer equity, derive useful insights into customer relationship management, use customer lifetime as a basis for market segmentation, and propose a way to use ICE to measure the value of a firm.

The second part analyzes two different customer retention programmes implemented by the firm. And also the third part studied customer lifetime and inter-purchase times simultaneously, explicitly accounting for the relationship between them. Their results showed that when a customer was at a higher risk of leaving the firm, he/she was less likely to purchase from it. Overall, the results showed strong evidence in support of modeling the two processes simultaneously.

Liz *et al.* (2003)[26] in their study entitled "How E-CRM Can Enhance Customer Loyalty" highlighted that Internet-based companies need to remain competitive. One way of improving competitive advantage was to attract more customers and increase customer retention; for example, by developing long-term, secure relationships between the buyers and sellers. Little empirical research had been conducted on the link between customer relationship management and customer loyalty within an Internet, or e-commerce, context. This study provided evidence of how to improve planning for customer management by presenting and testing a conceptual model of the process by which the implementation of electronic relationship marketing (e-CRM), could enhance loyalty. While building the research framework, price sensitivity was found to be a primary confounding element on loyalty and was included in the study for control. An exploratory study of Internet retailers, e-retailers, and their customers was conducted and the findings revealed that e-retail companies (with CD, DVD, video and book products) should consider customers' perceptions of relationship marketing efforts, as they were fundamental to enhancing customer loyalty and that an enhancement of customer loyalty reduces price sensitivity.

Ritter, Thomas and Achim Walter (2003)[27] in their study entitled "Relationship - Specific Antecedents of Customer Involvement in New Product Development: Research in New Product Development (NPD)" have identified customer involvement as an important means to accelerate product development, to reduce development costs, and to enhance new product value. This is grounded in the wealth of customers' knowledge due to their product and market experiences. Therefore, customer involvement may provide access to innovative product ideas, new technologies, market information, and development capabilities that the manufacturer lacks in-house. While much has been written about the potential benefits of partnering with customers, only a few researchers have attempted to document empirically the factors that foster customer involvement in NPD. This study examines the influence of relationship management tasks on customer involvement in NPD using data from more than 233 supplier-customer relationships. Their findings suggest that five relationship management tasks have a strong impact on customer involvement in NPD. Relationship sponsoring, technological consulting, information brokering, representing interests, and coordinating cooperative activities are crucial for integrating customers into NPD processes.

Keith Fletcher (2003)[28] in his study entitled "Consumer Power and Privacy: The Changing Nature of CRM" pointed out the difficulties that privacy concerns are creating for the growth of e-business and customer relationship management (CRM). The paper introduces the concept that the changing nature of consumer power is an essential element in ensuring the success of relationship building. The paper argues that consumers should be studied using two dimensions of knowledge and attitudes towards CRM to create a privacy grid. Four segments are discussed in terms of customers' reactions to information exchange and CRM activities. This grid is then translated into four distinct types of market situations and marketing strategies to be considered by CRM practitioners and recommendations made.

Thomas *et al.* (2004)[29]in their study entitled 'Recapturing Lost Customers' highlighted that for both academics and practitioners, the dominant focus of customer relationship management has been customer retention. The authors assert that customer win-back should also be an important part of a customer relationship management strategy. Customer win-back focuses on the reinitiating and management of relationships with customers who have lapsed or defected from a firm. In some cases, firms engage in extensive efforts to reacquire lapsed customers or defectors, and a common tactic is lowering the price to reacquire a customer. This investigation goes beyond the reacquisition pricing strategy and also examines the optimal pricing strategy when the customer has decided to reinitiate the relationship. By simultaneously modeling reacquisition and duration of the second tenure with the firm, the authors determine that the optimal pricing strategy for their application involves a low reacquisition price and higher prices when customers have been reacquired. In addition to pricing strategy, they also discussed the implications of their findings for targeting lapsed customers for reacquisition.

Bettis-Outland, E. Harriette (2004)[30] in his research work entitled "Critical Roles of Information Overload, Information Quality, and Perceived Information Distortion on Organisational Effectiveness: A Customer Relationship Management Perspective" opined that the research developed a model of organisational effectiveness, driven by certain characteristics of organisational information, and utilization of this information. Information characteristics included information overload, information quality, and perceived information distortion. Information utilization refers to the managerial processes of strategic consensus and responsiveness, which specify how the information is used organisation-wide.

This research takes place in the context of the selling organisation's customer relationship management system. Customer relationship management describes the technology and methods used by organisations to document, analyze, and build strategy aimed at improving the relationship between the firm and its customers. Information gathered in a CRM environment is contrasted with non-CRM information to determine differences in how each type of information is utilized within the organisation.

The Market Orientation and Learning Organisation concepts are integrated and extended with the development of the CRM-Organisational Effectiveness (COE) model. The COE model suggests that certain information characteristics (overload, quality, and distortion) occur during information generation and dissemination, then directly impact the managerial processes of strategic consensus and responsiveness. In turn, these managerial processes directly impact organisational effectiveness. The findings are discussed and recommendations for future research are offered.

CRM IN B2B MODEL

Morley, Roy (2004)[31] in his work entitled "Customer-based Antecedents of Satisfaction and Dissatisfaction in Business-to-business Services" highlights that the motivation for this research is the identification, from the customers' viewpoint, of the antecedents of satisfaction and dissatisfaction in a business-to-business (B2B) service environment at the service encounter. The research spans both services marketing and services operations. Previous work in the area of services quality, satisfaction and dissatisfaction has not adequately identified what drives satisfaction and dissatisfaction in the B2B environment.

This study seeks to fill that gap.The findings demonstrated that the antecedents of satisfaction and dissatisfaction in the B2B environment were quite different from what anecdotal evidence might suggest. Indeed, the results differed significantly from an earlier study undertaken in the business-to-consumer (B2C) environment. Customers base their perceptions of service organisations on interactions, or encounters, with the service provider that lead to satisfaction, dissatisfaction, or a neutral state. These customer-based assessments of service quality and satisfaction, dissatisfaction, or neutrality will lead to a loyal customer and retention, or defection of that customer, particularly in situations with low switching costs.

The objective of this study is to identify the role and magnitude of ten dimensions of service quality as antecedents of satisfaction (satisfiers) and dissatisfaction (dissatisfiers) in a B2B service environment, from the perspective of the customer. The results of this study indicated that some dimensions of service quality are associated with satisfaction; some are more aligned with dissatisfaction; and some are associated to varying degrees with both satisfaction and dissatisfaction. The results of the qualitative methodology agreed closely with the results of the quantitative methodology. The most important dimensions are responsiveness and understanding the customer.

The study was conducted with commercial B2B customers of a major Canadian bank and is only concerned with high contact service situations, typically with one-on-one delivery, but not Internet or equipment-based delivery. It is anticipated that the results of this study may be generalizable to other high contact, people-based, B2B service providers.

Henry, Euston, (2004)[32] in his work entitled "Customer Perceptions of Satisfaction of Solution Technology Services" highlight the perceptions of business customers about satisfaction with their solution technology suppliers. The study used the SERVQUAL perception-expectation instrument to survey U.S. banks, investment brokerages, a division of the U.S. Army, and insurance companies with assets of at least one billion dollars to identify what they believed suppliers might consider for addressing customer satisfaction with technology services. The study hypothesized that improved services would improve satisfaction. The findings suggested that there was little relationship between the perception-expectation and satisfaction although users expected improved services. The instrument's gap-scores model failed to account for the users' high expectations and may not be applicable for researching this technology sector service issues. Further research is necessary to understand customers' requirements.

Torres, Antonio (2004)[33] in his study entitled "Factors Influencing Customer Relationship Management (CRM) Performance in Agribusiness Firms" said that the objective of their study was to identify the activities/behaviours/outcomes that comprised and impacted Customer Relationship Management programmes of agribusinesses and identify key differences across the core set of activities/behaviours/outcomes and firm demographic variables by firm size (small, medium, and large), general market segments served (crop, livestock, services, and diversified), and by primary position in the distribution channel (direct, one-level, and complex) of agribusinesses. The final objective was to develop taxonomy of agribusiness firms based on the perceived performance of their CRM programmes. The analysis identified three distinct groups; which were named Leaders, Emerging Leaders, and Underachievers. For each group, a narrative profile was developed that described their activities/behaviours/outcomes and highlighted differences in these core elements across firms. Overall, results suggest that large firms have a resource advantage to develop and maintain customer relationships and encountered fewer challenges to making the best use of customer data in an information system/database.

Choo, Ho Jung (2004)[34] in his study entitled "The efficacy of consumer-employee and consumer-retailer relationships in predicting store loyalty among Korean consumers" highlight that relationship marketing literature emphasizes that a stable relationship between consumers and marketers is beneficial to both parties. This perspective has been adopted in the service literature, and many service marketing researchers have investigated the effects of consumer-service provider relationships on business performance. This study found that employee service, retail operations, retail facilities, and business ethics positively affect the consumer-employee relationship, while only merchandise quality and retail operations positively affect the Consumer-Retailer Relationship. The results indicate that it is the consumer-employee relationship that is directly affected by various retail attributes; however, this consumer-employee relationship ultimately affects the consumer-retailer relationship. A two-group comparison SEM analysis found that trust in employees becomes more important in the consumer-employee relationship for consumers with a longer relationship with the department store, and store commitment was more important for long-term consumers in the consumer-retailer relationship. Marketing implications for retailers are discussed.

Bernstal, Janet Bigham (2004)[35] in his study entitled "Good Customer Retention Demands Both Communication and Control" highlights the Customer retention is a big deal in all industries these days, especially when the Direct Marketing Association says that you lose 10 per cent to 40 per cent of your customers every year. To reduce the attrition rate, Customer Communications Group (CCG) of Denver, a company that provides CRM, strategic marketing and data-driven research services, has developed some new customer programmes based on two features: communication and control. The CCG has developed a communications scheme that looks at transactional data over the course of a year, as well as other information from surveys and so forth. This is downloaded monthly from the bank. From that, a segmentation system is designed to talk to the customer in an appropriate manner.

CRM IN E-BUSINESS

Horn *et al.* (2005)[36] in their study entitled "Determinant Elements of Customer Relationship Management in E-business" investigated the composition of customer relationship management (CRM) in e-business by examining the possible elements that determine different aspects of the relationship between customers and e-businesses. A web-based CRM survey of 38 items, constructed from SERVQUAL (service quality instrument), SITEQUAL (website service quality instrument) and literature findings, was completed by 200 customer contact professionals. The results of the study indicate that customers perceive three main dimensions of relationship attributes of e-business (general CRM, personalization and privacy) and that all three significantly contribute to customer attitude. These findings support the importance of including relational-type e-business attributes when investigating interactions between customers and e-business. The study concludes with related implications and design guidelines to enhancing customer perception of e-business.

Srinivasan *et al.* (2005)[37] in their study entitled "Strategic Firm Commitments and Rewards for Customer Relationship Management in Online Retailing" revealed that Academic studies offer a generally positive portrait of the effect of customer relationship management (CRM) on firm performance, but practitioners question its value. The authors argue that a firm's strategic commitments may be an overlooked organisational factor that influences the rewards for a firm's investments in CRM. Using the context of online retailing, the authors consider the effects of two key strategic commitments of online retailers on the performance effect of CRM: their bricks-and-mortar experience and their online entry timing. They test the proposed model with a multi method approach that uses manager ratings of firm CRM and strategic commitments and third-party customers' ratings of satisfaction from 106 online retailers. The findings indicate that firms with moderate bricks-and-mortar experience are better able to leverage CRM for superior customer satisfaction outcomes than firms with either low or high bricks-and-mortar experience. Likewise, firms with moderate online experience are better able to leverage CRM into superior customer satisfaction outcomes than firms with either low or high online experience. These findings help resolve disparate results about the value of CRM, and they establish the importance of examining CRM within the strategic context of the firm.

Thoams *et al.* (2005),[38] in their study entitled "Managing Marketing Communications with Multi-channel Customers" highlighted marketing communications process that uses customer relationship management ideas for multi-channel retailers. The authors describe and then demonstrate the process with enterprise-level data from a major U.S. retailer with multiple channels. On the basis of the results, the authors develop an initial marketing communications strategy for the retailer.

Vyas, Preeta Hemang and Vikalpa (2005),[39] in their study entitled "Incentive Outlay Ratios in Fast Moving Consumer Goods Sector in India" pointed out that the Inflationary trends in the economy have led to increased media costs forcing many companies to increase their expenditure on sales promotion activities. It has been recognized that well-planned sales promotion activities have a strategic role to play in brand building and enhancing customer loyalty. This study examines the nature of schemes offered in the fast moving consumer goods (FMCG) category, finds out the ratio of incentive and outlay (which the consumer is expected to make/pay to avail sales promotion offers), explores the relationships, finds out the rationale behind these offers, and provides guidelines to managers designing sales promotion activities.

Joan L. Anderson *et al.* (2005)[40], in their study entitled, "Customer Relationship Management in Retailing: A Content Analysis of Retail Trade Journals" stated that their research was to increase knowledge and understanding of how retailers use business intelligence and data mining tools to implement customer relationship management (CRM) in retailing. Specific objectives were to (1) identify organisation and infrastructure requirements for CRM effectiveness, (2) identify CRM objectives and goals of retail companies, (3) identify data mining tools utilized by retailers to perform CRM functions, and (4) identify CRM strategies used by retail companies. Retailers goals/objectives and strategies focused on marketing, customer service, understanding customers through data analysis and increasing acquisition and retention through customer loyalty programmes. Data mining tools identified supported marketing and customer analysis efforts. Findings provide insight into the challenges retailers face as they implement a more customer-centric business strategy.

Jaakko Sinisalo *et al.* (2005)[41] in their study entitled "Initiation Stage of a Mobile Customer Relationship Management" stress that Customer Relationship Management (CRM) has become a topic of major importance. However, the mobile medium as an element of CRM is rarely taken into consideration. The aim of the present study is to integrate these two important areas by providing an understanding of how to utilize the mobile medium in CRM. The main purpose of this study is to build an empirically grounded framework of the initiation stage of

Mobile Customer Relationship Management (mCRM) in retailing. The empirical part of the study employs a single-case study method. In detail, there is a major retailer involved that adopted mCRM and utilized the means of mobile marketing to activate customers to start a dialogue via mobile phone. The main results of the study indicate that while there are a lot of uncertainties related to adopting mCRM, the mobile medium may be an effective complement to traditional CRM. The paper finally presents contributions, limitations and avenues for further research.

CRM STRATEGIES

Al-Shuridah, Obaid Mobarak (2005)[42] in his study entitled "Customer Intention as the Key to Successful CRM Implementation: Empirical Insights from an SEM Application" point out that in order to improve customer relationships, firms rely heavily on technology-based solutions that CRM provides. However, studies and business reports estimate that 30 per cent to 75 per cent of CRM initiatives fail to achieve their goals. This high incidence of failure is often attributed to firm-related factors (e.g., lack of cultural readiness) or technology (e.g., software incompatibility with firm-specific needs). This study contributes to this debate by highlighting several customer-related factors that are critical to CRM programmes implementations.

Zablah, Alex Ricardo (2005)[43] in his study entitled "A Communication Based Perspective on Customer Relationship Management (CRM)" highlighted that although little empirical evidence exists to support this contention, the extant literature suggests that firms can potentially achieve two types of benefits from developing a CRM orientation: (1) increased efficiency in the allocation of resources destined for relationship building and maintenance activities, and (2) enhanced exchange relationship outcomes through the provision of superior customer value. A conceptual model of "CRM success" was advanced and tested utilizing data from both customers and their providers.

Thakur, Ramendra (2005)[44] in his study entitled "Customer satisfaction, behaviour intention, attitude, and knowledge: Focus on the antecedents of relationship share in the context of Customer Relationship Management (CRM)" opines that in today's highly competitive business world, customer relationship management (CRM) is emerging as a core marketing activity. Studies have indicated that it costs six times more to acquire new customers than to retain an existing one. Hence, many firms are devoting more attention to maintain and develop relationships with customers, which is likely to increase the Customers' Willingness to Engage in Relationship (CWER) with the firm and increase the Customer Relationship Share (CRS) of that firm. The findings of the study also indicate that CWER depends on customers' attitude toward the firm and that attitude depends on customers' knowledge and belief about the firm's CRM programme.

Steffes, Erin Marshall (2005)[45] in his study entitled "Establishing the Link between Relationship Marketing, Customer Profitability and Customer Lifetime" highlights that the customer relationship management has become an important area of research in recent times. There is paucity of research that looks at the customer profit and customer longevity implications of customer acquisition and retention strategies. Using a proprietary data set from the credit card industry, he first examines the profit implications and second examine the customer lifetime implications of different modes of acquisition of customers. Further, he examines the role of two popular customer retention strategies, namely, reward cards and affinity cards in driving both customer profitability and longevity. Surprisingly, he finds that in the dataset, customers with reward cards and affinity cards are less profitable than those customers without access to these retention strategies. However, he finds that affinity customers have longer lifetimes than non-affinity customers. He also finds that Internet and direct mail communications are more profitable than telemarketing and direct selling in customer acquisition. These results have important managerial implications for resource allocation in acquisition and retention strategies.

Lin, Yaonan (2005)[46] in his study entitled “Information Privacy Concerns in the Customer Relationship Management Context: A Comparison of Consumer Attitudes in the United States, China, and Taiwan” aimed to develop a holistic conceptual model of consumers’ information privacy concerns in the Customer Relationship Management context and to conduct an empirical test of the model. Also, the focus of this study is to investigate how the cultural differences influence consumers’ attitudes about their information privacy and to find differences in levels of consumers’ information privacy concerns in the U.S., China, and Taiwan. The final point of this study is to find the relationships among the variables in the information privacy concerns model. The results showed that there are significant differences in information privacy concerns among the respondents from the U.S., China, and Taiwan. Furthermore, a path analysis was used to examine the links in the model. There were strong relationships among the above seven variables. The study results indicated that consumers’ trust and knowledge about CRM influence their information privacy concerns directly. The study results suggested that marketers should understand their customers’ information privacy concerns in the CRM context, so that they could provide efficient CRM service for targeted customers.

Bang and Jounghae (2005)[47] in their study entitled “Understanding Customer Relationship Management from Managers’ and Customers’ Perspective: Exploring the Implications of CRM fit, Market Orientation, and Market Knowledge Competence” highlight that the Customer

Relationship Management (CRM) has received a lot of attention and come to occupy a central place as a vital strategy in organisations. The findings highlight the importance of well-designed CRM processes and of understanding the perspectives of customers in relationship building. The results imply that managers should be aware of the different effects of each stage of CRM and of planning appropriate strategies for members and nonmembers to generate and reinforce satisfaction and commitment.

Hou, Yonghai (2005)[48] in their study entitled "Service Quality of Online Apparel Retailers and its Impact on Customer Satisfaction, Customer Trust and Customer Loyalty" discussed that the rapid growth of Internet market and customers' increased savviness in using information technology have significantly changed the landscape of retail business. Customers are inclined to accept the changes and keep their eyes on the benefits they can obtain from these creative online service platforms. Apparel product, an important category in offline retailing, has also become a more and more active sector in the online market. There is a need for both practitioners and academics to understand what are the antecedent factors of service quality which consumers perceived and how the perceptions of service quality influences customers' satisfaction, trust, and loyalty.

Wouter Buckinx and Dirk Van den Poel (2005)[49] in their study entitled "Customer Base Analysis: Partial Defection of Behaviourally Loyal Clients in a Non-contractual FMCG Retail Setting" explained how the Customer Relationship Management (CRM) enjoys increasing attention as a countermeasure to switching behaviour of customers. Because foregone profits of (partially) defected customers can be significant, an increase of the retention rate can be very profitable. In this paper they focus on the treatment of a company's most behaviourally loyal customers in a non-contractual setting. They build a model in order to predict partial defection by behaviourally loyal clients using three classification techniques: Logistic regression, Automatic Relevance Determination (ARD) Neural Networks and Random Forests. Moreover, additional variables such as the length of customer relationship, mode of payment, buying behaviour across categories, usage of promotions and brand purchase behaviour are shown in this study.

William J Lundstrom and Robert F Wright (2005)[50] in their study entitled "The CRM-physician Interface: Toward a Model of Physician Relationship Building" had the experience of addressing several conferences focusing on how to develop and use customer relationship management (CRM) in the pharmaceutical field to increase productivity, sales and profitability. Indeed, CRM is both a tool, and a perspective, that involves a long process in developing a true relationship. Unfortunately, more often than not, the CRM model employed by pharmaceutical management is that of using the tool rather than developing the relationship. The ultimate goal of customer relationship management is to tie the customer to the brand of company. The link between brand equity and customer relationship equity (CRE) is seen as one preceding the other. Brand equity and brand management is a significant subset of the CRM model and plays a significant role in its link to CRE. CRM is not customer relationship building or creating CRE. It is a technology that can aid in the process on building relationships, but it is not relationship building.

Jayachandran *et al.* (2005)[51] in their study entitled "The Role of Relational Information Processes and Technology Use in Customer Relationship Management" point out that many firms have invested in customer relationship management (CRM) technology in the hope of discriminating between profitable and unprofitable customers, providing customized service, and obtaining higher customer retention. However, the results of using CRM technology have been mixed, and this has created substantial concern about its viability and effectiveness. The unease with CRM technology use is similar to the disillusionment that firms encountered in the late 1980s regarding the use of information technology (IT) to automate business activities. This study identifies the key relational information processes that should be implemented by firms that opt to pursue CRM. Delineation of relational information processes enables managers to track and evaluate the information routines relevant for CRM.

Compton, Jason (2005)[52] in his study entitled "CRM is a Journey Not a Destination" highlight that shepherding a CRM project from inception to the first pilot and the eventual training and enterprise wide rollout is no small task. Coordinating important customer-centric changes in sales, marketing, and service takes time, far more than it takes to flip a switch on a database or distribute an on-demand sales-automation Website. Aventail, a provider of network encryption and virtual private network products, began its CRM implementation in 1997. The company had to concentrate on the same basic principles of effective sales communication and support even as the target customers fluctuated wildly. Over the past decade many financial services firms have seized on CRM strategies in an attempt to market more products to more people.

Nelson *et al.* (2006)[53] in their study entitled 'Customer Satisfaction with Electronic Service Encounters' emphasized that Customer Relationship Management is an integral component of business strategy for on-line service providers. This paper investigates the aspects of on-line transactions in electronic retailing that are most likely to satisfy or dissatisfy customers, thereby increasing or decreasing the likelihood of building and maintaining relationships with them. For this study, 513 respondents reported behaviours, perceptions, beliefs, events, features, characteristics, attributes, and situations that expressed their satisfaction or dissatisfaction with electronic service encounters. The study found that the characteristics and behaviours of customer-contact employees play an important role in on-line service encounters.

CRM IN RETAILING

Mary Conway *et al.* (2006)[54] in their study entitled "Creating Effective Customer Relationships in Not-for-profit Retailing" highlight that Ten Thousand Villages (a not-for-profit organisation with retail operations in US and Canada that pays Third World artisans fair market value for their works in terms of its retailing and customer relationship management (CRM) strategies. The authors present an analysis of Ten Thousand Villages' retail stores to assess if and how CRM might be successfully implemented. The analysis considers the use of a volunteer retail sales force and how volunteers might successfully interface with customers.

Meyer-Waarden *et al.* (2006)[55] in their study entitled "The Impact of Loyalty Programmes on Repeat Purchase Behaviour" highlighted how to contribute to a better knowledge about the impact of retailing loyalty programmes on repeat purchase behaviour. It is based on the Behaviour Scan single-source panel which has been crossed with the store data base of a French retailer. They implemented the multinomial Dirichlet model, in order to test the impact of loyalty programmes on the general market structure. The double jeopardy phenomenon is present and loyalty programmes do not substantially change market structures. When all companies have loyalty programmes, the market is characterized by an absence of change of the competitive situation.

Pistelak and Petr (2006)[56] in their study entitled "Selling Banks is the same as Selling Soap: Applying Fast-Moving Consumer Goods Best Marketing Practices to the Banking Industry in Central and Eastern Europe" highlight that attempts to market financial services as fast-moving consumer goods products are rather rare in the traditional banking industry. eBank, a small retail and SME bank in the Czech Republic, applied the FMCG marketing approach with great success. Long-time FMCG marketer, Petr Pistelak, explains the basic principles of FMCG marketing and shows how they were applied to triple the revenue of a small bank in less than three years, while bringing the once struggling bank into profitability.

Chakravorti, Samit (2006)[57] in his dissertation entitled "Customer Relationship Management: A Content Analysis of Issues and Best Practices" highlights the study of customer relationship management theory and practice. Customer Relationship Management (CRM) is a business strategy whereby companies build strong relationships with existing and prospective customers with the goal of increasing organisational profitability. It is also a learning process involving managing change in processes, people, and technology. CRM implementation and its ramifications are also not completely understood as evidenced by the high number of failures in CRM implementation in organisations and the resulting disappointments. The goal of this dissertation is to study emerging issues and trends in CRM, including the effect of computer software and the accompanying new management processes on organisations, and the dynamics of the alignment of marketing, sales and services, and all other functions responsible for delivering customers a satisfying experience. Results show that there is a lack of holistic thinking and discussion of CRM in both academics and industry which is required to understand how the people, process, and technology in CRM impact each other to affect successful implementation. Industry has to get its heads around CRM and holistically understand how these important dimensions affect each other. Only then will organisational learning occur, and overtime result in superior processes leading to strong profitable customer relationships and a hard to imitate competitive advantage.

Baohong (2006)[58] in his study entitled "Technology Innovation and Implications for Customer Relationship Management" highlight that the recent development of CRM technology calls for rigorous research to better understand the nature of this emerging industry and to help design the best marketing programmes. A better understanding of the development of demand has important implications for the design of cross-selling campaign strategy. The emergence of data-mining technology calls for a substantial amount of research to develop statistical learning rules for adaptive machine learning and automated implementation of CRM. For a firm with the goal of maximizing long-term profit, CRM should be formulated as a stochastic dynamic control problem under demand uncertainty with the firm as the decision maker which makes dynamic marketing intervention decisions such as pricing, channel strategy or cross-selling campaign.

Dale Wilson (2006)[59] in his study entitled "Developing New Business Strategies in B2B Markets by Combining CRM Concepts and Online Databases" illustrates how online databases, available from commercial vendors, can be used as the foundation for developing new business strategies. Emphasis is placed on the use of customer relationship management (CRM) ideas to identify new prospective customers for a high-tech B2B firm. Specifically, the concept of customer lifetime value was used to evaluate current customers and match their profiles with the profiles of new prospects from the database. Once high-quality new prospects were identified and prioritized, the company's sales force had a much clearer path to follow towards success. This study contributes to the competitive strategy literature by documenting the successful use of a CRM approach to develop marketing strategies and tactics for a B2B firm that is seeking growth by acquiring new customers.

Wann Yih Wu, Hsi-An Shih and Hui-Chun Chan (2008)[60] in their study entitled "A Study of Customer

Relationship Management Activities and Marketing Tactics for Hypermarkets on Membership Behaviour" highlighted that is the current retail environment, relationship management activities and marketing tactics play a predominant role because of the increased importance that consumers attach to the relational properties of their interactions with retailers. As a result, substantial competitive advantage development is required in order to establish effective membership relations. Further, as a result of the vigorous development and competition of the Taiwanese hypermarket, establishment of the extant membership relationship becomes a key method of building competitive advantage in the hypermarket. Therefore, this study investigates the interaction of membership relationship management activities and marketing tactics in the hypermarket through perceived relationship-investment linking; understood member's psychological factors that promote customer value; allowing industries and customers to establish a good membership relationship; and finally, the influences of relationship quality and membership behaviour.

REFERENCES

1. Parasuraman, Zeithaml, Valarie A Berry and Leonard.L (1985) *Journal of Marketing*, Fall 85, Vol. 49, Issue 4, pp. 41-50.
2. McDermott, Michael, Choi and Tim (1997) *Journal of Marketing Management*, January-April 97, Vol. 13, Issue 1-3, pp. 195-217.
3. Bolton, R.L. and Katherine (1999), *Journal of Marketing Research*, Vol. 36, Issue 2, pp. 171-186.
4. Castelo, Pita and Jose (2000), Unpublished Thesis, Universidad Complutense de Madrid, Spain, p. 307.
5. Zahay and Debra, L. (2000), "Aligning Strategy and Customer Information for Performance in Business Markets", University of Illinois at Urbana-Champaign, p. 211.
6. Zakheim, Betty (2000), America's Network, Duluth: Vol. 104, Iss. 18, p. 89.
7. Foss and Stone (2001), Relationship Marketing.

8. Hagy and Richard Alan (2001), Ph.D., University of Southern California, p. 130.

9. Atkin, Thomas S. (2001), Unpublished Thesis, Michigan State University, 2001, p. 196.

10. Verhoef, Peter.C, Franses, Philip Hans, Hoekstra, Janny.C, (2001), *Journal of Retailing*, Vol. 77, Issue 3, pp. 359-368.

11. Garden (2001), *Direct Marketing*. Garden City: October, Vol. 64, Issue. 6, p. 12.

12. Yu, Larry (2001), *MIT Sloan Management Review*, Cambridge: Summer. Vol. 42, Issue 4, pp. 18-19.

13. Feinberg, R.A, Kadam R, Hokama L, Kim T (2002), *International Journal of Retail & Distribution Management*, Vol. 30, pp. 470-481.

14. Xue, Mei (2002), Unpublished Thesis, University of Pennsylvania, p. 205.

15. Wayment, Tawna (2002), Unpublished Thesis, Utah State University, 2002.

16. Li Kam Wa and Peter (2002), Concordia University, Canada.

17. Severt, Denver Eugene (2002), Virginia Polytechnic Institute and State University, 2002, p. 118.

18. Cho, Yooncheong (2002), Rutgers The State University of New Jersey, Newark, p. 175.

19. Treytl, Kristina Joy (2002), San Jose State University, p. 33.

20. Paul Krill (2002), *InfoWorld, San Mateo:* Feb 4, Vol. 24, Iss. 5, p. 37.

21. Payant & W. Randall (2003), *Journal of Bank Cost & Management Accounting*, Vol. 16, Issue 3, pp. 41-47.

22. Wu, Wei (2003), Unpublished Thesis, Concordia University, Canada, p. 130.

23. DeFazio, Vincent James (2003), University of Phoenix, 141 p..

24. Saini, Amit (2003), Ph.D Thesis Washington State University, 2003, p. 152.

25. Singh, Siddharth Shekhar (2003), Ph.D Thesis, Northwestern University, p. 179.

26. Liz, Lee-Kelley, David Gilbert and Robin Mannicom (2003), Marketing Intelligence & Planning. Bradford, Vol. 21, Iss. 4/5, p. 239.

27. Ritter, Thomas and Achim Walter (2003), *International Journal of Technology Management*. Geneva, Vol. 26, Iss. 5, 6, p. 482.

28. Fletcher Keith (2003), *International Journal of Advertising, Eastbourne*, 2003, Vol. 22, Iss. 2, p. 249.

29. Thomas, Jacquelyn S, Blattberg, Robert C, Fox and Edward J (2004), Journal of Marketing Research, Vol. 41, Issue 1, pp. 31-45.

30. Bettis-Outland (2004), E. Harriette, Unpublished Thesis, Georgia State University, p. 185.

31. Morley, Roy (2004), Unpublished Thesis, The University of Western Ontario (Canada), p. 255.

32. Henry, Euston M (2004), Unpublished Thesis, University of Phoenix, p. 210.

33. Torres, Antonio (2004), Unpublished Thesis, Purdue University, p. 285.

34. Choo, Ho Jung (2004), Unpublished Thesis, Michigan State University, p. 159.

35. Bernstal, Janet Bigham (2004), ABA Bank Marketing, Washington: May, Vol. 36, Iss. 4, p. 23.

36. Horn, D, Feinberg R and Salvendy.G (2005), Behaviour and Information Technology, Vol. 24, Issue 2, pp. 101-109.

37. Srinivasan, Raji, Moorman and Christine (2005), *Journal of Marketing*, Vol. 69, Issue 4, pp. 193-200.

38. Thoams, Jacquelyn S, Sullivan and Ursula Y (2005), *Journal of Marketing*, Vol. 69, Issue 4, pp. 239-251.

39. Vyas Preeta Hemang and Vikalpa (2005), *The Journal for Decision Makers*, 2005, Vol. 30, Issue 4, pp. 39-47.

40. Joan L. Anderson, Laura D, Jolly and Ann E. Fairhurst, Washington State University, USA, 2005.

41. Jaakko Sinisalo, Finland Jari Salo, Finland Matti Leppanieme, Finland Heikki Karjaluoto (2005), University of Oulu.

42. Al-Shuridah, Obaid Mobarak (2005), Unpublished Thesis, Southern Illinois University at Carbondale, p. 225.

43. Zablah, Alex Ricardo (2005), Unpublished Thesis, Georgia State University, p. 261.

44. Thakur, Ramendra (2005), Unpublished Thesis, Southern Illinois University at Carbondale, p. 108.

45. Steffes and Erin Marshall (2005), Unpublished Thesis, The University of Texas at Dallas, p. 194.

46. Lin, Yaonan (2005), Unpublished Thesis, Golden Gate University, p. 170.

47. Bang and Jounghae (2005), Unpublished Thesis University of Rhode Island, p. 165.

48. Hou, Yonghai (2005), Unpublished Thesis, The University of North Carolina at Greensboro, p. 236.

49. Wouter Buckinx and Dirk Van den Poel (2005), *European Journal of Operational Research*, Amsterdam, Vol. 164, Issue. 1, p. 252.

50. William J Lundstrom, Robert F Wright (2005), *Journal of Medical Marketing*, London, Vol. 5, Issue. 4, pp. 316-323.

51. Jayachandran, Satish , Subhash Sharma, Peter Kaufman, Pushkala Raman (2005), *Journal of Marketing*. Chicago, Vol. 69, Iss. 4, p. 177.

52. Compton, Jason (2005), *Customer Relationship Management*, Medford, Vol. 9, Iss. 5, pp. 38-42.

53. Massad, Nelson, Heckman, Robert, Crowston and Kevin (2006), *International Journal of Electronic Commerce*, Vol. 10, Issue 4, pp. 73-104.

54. Doto-on, Mary Conway, Joyce, Mary, Manolis and Chris (2006), *International Journal of Non-profit Voluntary Sector Marketing*, Vol. 11, Issue 4, pp. 319-333.

55. Meyer-Waarden, Lars, Benavent, Christophe (2006), *Journal of Marketing Management*, Vol. 22, Issue ½, pp. 61-88.

56. Pistelak & Petr (2006), *Journal of Financial Services Marketing*, Vol. 11, Issue 1, pp. 72-84.

57. Chakravorti, Samit (2006), Unpublished Thesis, Florida International University, p. 162.

58. Baohong Sun (2006), *Marketing Science*, Linthicum: November/ December, Vol. 25, Iss. 6, p. 594.

59. Dale Wilson (2006), *Competitiveness Review*, Indiana, 2006, Vol. 16, Issue 1, pp. 38-43.

60. Wann Yih Wu, Hsi-An Shih, Hui-Chun Chan (2008). *The Business Review*, Cambridge. Hollywood, Summer, Vol. 10, Iss. 1, pp. 89-94.

Conceptual Framework of Customer Relationship Management

Customer Relationship Management is an integration of business processes and technologies employed to satisfy the needs of a customer during any given interaction. The concept of CRM involves acquisition analysis and use of knowledge about the customers with a view to effectively sell more and more goods and services. The implementation of a customer-centred strategy and re-engineering the current customer interaction of the process of the organisation will help in retaining the existing customers and attracting new ones. Basically, CRM is considered as a business strategy and not as a technology. Pairing the CRM tools with the right management attitudes not only helps the firm generate and retain customers; but also provides it with a competitive advantage. Implementation of CRM will increase the delight of the customers and make them stay longer and be loyal to the organisation for a longer period. It can be recognized as an initial step towards the attainment of partnership marketing.

Customer Relationship Management (CRM) is a strategy adopted by business firms in recent years and includes the formulation of methodologies and tools that help businesses manage customer relationships in an organized way. The CRM processes are extremely helpful in identifying and targeting the best customers of the business firm, and generating quality sales leads, as well as in the planning and implementation of marketing campaigns with definite goals and objectives. The processes involved in CRM can help the firm maintain a customized relationship with the customers for creating higher-level customer satisfaction and offering the finest customer service. The CRM also endows the employees of the organisations with the information they need to know about their customers' wants and needs, and to build a long-term sustained relationship between the firm and its customers.

Customer Relationship Management (CRM) has become immensely popular because of the promise it holds for organisations. The CRM provides competitive advantage to the organisations at a time when product, price and place differentiations are fast disappearing from the marketplace. Various organisations have successfully implemented CRM projects and it has become the new mantra that is being chanted from many a boardroom across the globe. Many people firmly believe that CRM is a very valuable organisational strategy that can transform the organisations by providing great opportunities and has come to stay. They point out the benefits reaped by organisations that successfully implemented CRM. However, some people disagree and are of the view that CRM is a fad, which is already on the decline. Assessing this issue, whether CRM is a useful organisational strategy that is capable of providing immense opportunities or a passing fad that failed to deliver, needs in-depth understanding of CRM as an organisational strategy, right from its origin and why CRM has become so popular. Further, it also needs very deep insights into the role that technology plays in CRM. In the light of this divided opinion on CRM, this chapter discusses comprehensively the origin and development of CRM philosophy, its features, and the reasons as to why some people started looking at CRM as a passing fad while others consider it as one of the most important organisational strategies and critically examine which view reflects the reality.

CUSTOMER MANAGEMENT — A HISTORICAL PERSPECTIVE

In the 1990s, CRM started attracting attention of academicians as well as practitioners from marketing and IT. A series of research conferences on various aspects of buyer-seller relationships were organized by the Center for Relationship Marketing at the Emory University (1994-2000).

Peter Drucker once said: "The true business of every company is to make and keep customers." The single most important factor for the success of any business enterprise is the customer. Every one knew this fact right from the time commercial activities started, but unfortunately the customer has never got his due. The main reason for this was that all along, the demand outstripped supply. The customer had to be content with what he had got. Another factor was, the customer was not aware if some thing better existed. The information available in the market was scanty and there were not many sources that could have given information about the service or product the customer was looking for. It was a sellers market. Henry Ford's famous quote "I can provide any color car as long as it is black" sums up the choices available to the customer. Organisations initially practised only selling and slowly learnt that selling alone was not enough to be successful but creating value to customers through mutual exchange was essential. Thus, the concept of selling gave way to marketing. Through marketing, organisations wanted to reach as many customers as possible and this led to the concept of mass marketing. This strategy also failed, as organisations did not cater for the individual needs of the customer, presuming that all the customers had the same needs. However, during the 1950s, Japan, in spite of the defeat in the war, started capturing the world markets with their customer focused businesses. With increasing competition slowly things started changing in the US and Europe also. Thus started the customer-oriented programmes like 'Customer is always right' of 1940s formulated by Cesar Ritz, 'Customer satisfaction' of the 1970s, and 'Delighting the Customer' of 1990s. However, notwithstanding these slogans and increasing awareness about customer satisfaction, most of the organisations only paid lip service. With the failure of mass marketing, organisations started analyzing the data to find which of their products the customers were buying and in the process, the companies realized marketing their products to identified groups of customers, with similar needs and attributes yielded better results. This resulted in segmentation and target marketing.

Starting from 1980s the world and the business environment has undergone a sea change. With the disintegration of erstwhile USSR, world has become unipolar and trade blocks have disappeared or have lost their relevance. The second important development is deregulation and liberalization of economies by most countries. The third important development is the birth and growth of World Trade Organisation (WTO). The objective of WTO is to create a level playing field by lowering or removing trade barriers. The fourth and by far the most important development is the growth of Internet and Information Technologies. Internet has converted the world into a global market place, which never sleeps. It has not only changed the way businesses are conducted, but also created new ways of conducting businesses which are being collectively called as 'E-commerce'. All these developments contributed to the already advanced levels of competition in the market place. Globalization, deregulation, mergers and acquisitions mean subjecting businesses to rapidly changing forces. Only those organisations that are proactively changing in accordance with environmental changes are surviving and others are disappearing from the market. Internet has also transformed the society into a knowledge society. Plenty of information that is available on the Internet and accessible at the click of the mouse button has transformed a typical customer into an informed and powerful customer. Target marketing or segmented marketing worked well for some time, but with the increase in competition, globalization and demanding customers, target marketing too lost its effectiveness in the changed environment.

WHY CRM?

Traditionally businesses competed with others on the basis of price or the product features or by locating them at the places they were in demand. But in the present-day environment it is very difficult to compete on the basis of product features alone as so many technologies exist that facilitate near replication of functions and features, taking away the first mover advantage. Location used to be the oldest form of differentiator, but with e-commerce, the world has become smaller and this form of competitive advantage has also gone. But most important of all the changes is the shift from product related differentiation to service related differentiation. Customers are no longer satisfied with only products but expect the best possible after sales service. Customers can get any information about the product or service or any other issue in real time. With all the necessary information at his command, the customer has become very choosy and demanding. The scales now clearly tilt in favour of the customer.

Another factor is customer experience. Paul Greenberg (2001) author of popular *CRM at the Speed of Light* says:

> "When customers approach a business for a product or service, they also have an expectation associated with

their interest. The completed transaction leaves some kind of experience in the minds of the customers with regard to their expectation".

If the experience is pleasant the customer will repurchase otherwise he will not. Many surveys conclusively proved that repeat purchases are based on customer satisfaction and experience with that company.

In the face of highly demanding customer, increasing competition, mature markets, lowering product, price differentiation, a new reality had dawned on the businesses that, the only way to sustain revenues and growth is by treating the existing customers well and providing best experience to them. It costs a lot more to attract a new customer than retaining the existing ones. Further, a satisfied customer becomes the ambassador for the organisation where as a dissatisfied customer discourages many potential customers. Businesses clearly understood that the only way to survival and growth was by ensuring that the customer came back to them in future. A study found a strong correlation between customer satisfaction and customer retention. The study found that 95 per cent of the customers would come back if they perceived the service as "Excellent" and this dropped very significantly to 60 per cent if service level was perceived as `good'. This study also found that the revenues improved only when needs of the customers were well understood and the organisation fulfilled those needs effectively by offering suitable products or services. Organisations have become alive to these important findings and many of them are making sincere attempts aimed at serving the customer better. This is reflected in IBM's philosophy when they say that they did not sell products but sold solutions. CRM provides the competitive differentiation in near parity environment.

The CRM enables customer centric processes of identifying, acquiring, nurturing, retaining customers and developing life-long relationships with them by providing best possible service and satisfaction in the process of achieving organisational goals. Towards this end CRM aims at serving the customers on a one to one basis, reducing the intermediaries, continuously monitoring their needs, both stated and unstated, and providing services and products in alignment with those needs.

For a long time, marketers implemented their 4Ps strategy to attract and satisfy their target customers. But post-liberalization, the highly competitive and dynamic business environment has forced the businesses to think not only of attracting but also retaining their customers, especially profitable ones. This approach of businesses to build and maintain one-to-one life-long relationship with their large number of customers has led to the emergence of a new term CRM, which stands for CRM. This change in perspective is also supported by research findings that it costs up to 6-8 times more to attract a new customer than to retain an existing customer.

DEFINING CRM

The CRM, as concept, according to Scoot Fletcher, started gaining prominence in early 1997, and emerged as a management buzz and a topic of interest among business firms, media, software vendors, management gurus and academic institutions.

A Customer Relationship Management system, by its simplest definition, is a process to compile information that increases understanding of how to manage an organisation's relationships with its customers. In simple view, a CRM system consists of two dimensions, analysis and action.[1]

Robert Shaw (2001) says "CRM is an interactive process for achieving the optimum balance between corporate investments and the satisfaction of customer needs to generate the maximum profit."[2] CRM is a comprehensive strategy and process of acquiring, retaining and partnering with selective customers to create superior value for the company and the customer.

Starkey and Woodcock (1997) define CRM as "being a business philosophy, is an IT-enhanced value process, which identifies, develops, integrates and focuses the various competencies of the firm to the voice of the customers in order to deliver long-term superior customer value, at a profit, to well-identified existing and potential customer segments."[3]

According to Rigby, Reichheld and Schefter (2002), "CRM aligns business process with customer srategies to build customer loyalty and to increase profits overtime."[4] Thus CRM system effectively unifies and manages each stage of a complex sales process so that it is enjoyed by the truly customer-focused organisation.

In the words of Parvatiyar and Seth (2001), "CRM is a comprehensive strategy and process of acquiring, retaining, and partnering with selective customers to create superior value for the company and the customer." It is a process or methodology used to learn more about customers' needs and behaviours in order to develop stronger relationships with them. Greenleaf and Winer (2002) have explained CRM thus: "Customer Relationship Management is a business strategy to select and manage customers to optimize long-term value." CRM is a business approach that integrates people, processes, and technology to maximize the relations of an organisation with all types of customers.

THE NATURE OF CRM

The CRM is a business strategy and philosophy. The CRM is not technology. Organisations can practice CRM without technology. Organisations formulate different strategies for different areas to achieve their goals CRM is one of the many strategies. Organisations normally have many goals, like improvements in the bottom line or expanding markets overseas. Relevant strategies like product strategy, marketing strategy and CRM strategy are formulated to achieve these goals. Plans are the means of executing strategies. As a part of new product strategy one may plan an advertising bombardment. Objectives are measurable targets of each plan. It is through tactics that organisations achieve objectives. CRM technologies are implemented at this tactical level.

According to IBM, CRM essentially means two things. The first is 'Knowing Your Customer (KYC)' and the second is 'Appearing as one Entity' to the customer. Understanding the customer, his unique needs are at the core of CRM. Second is from the point of view of the customer an organisation is a single entity. Today a customer may contact the organisations in a number of ways from telephone to e-mail to call centre. Whenever a customer approaches an employee, by whatever means, the employee must have the history of the customer in front of him. The customer should not be made to repeat his details afresh whenever he speaks to a new person. Run of the mill organisations present a fragmented view to the customer. When a customer contacts a company with a problem, he is made to contact different people and at each place has to start afresh, and give his history. Nothing can be more frustrating to the customer. Companies must redesign their processes so as to project a unified view.

Successful CRM involves understanding customer value, consolidating customer information, and developing customer-centric infrastructure. Implementation of CRM needs leadership, strategy, technology and the right organisational culture. The CRM being an organisational strategy needs a long-term plan. Any long-term activity in an organisation needs total organisational commitment and also investment. CRM in the long-term will prove to be a bundle of opportunities for the organisations. Without CRM it is the organisations that are most likely to disappear from the market.

GROWTH OF CRM

The tremendous growth of interest and investments in CRM across the globe can be attributed to the following macro-environmental factors:

(a) Emergence of Service Economy

(b) Emergence of Market Economy

(c) Global Orientation of Business, and

(d) Aging Population of the Economically Advanced Economies.

SCHOOLS OF THOUGHT ON CRM

The growth of the practice of relationship marketing is supported by the growing research interest in different facets of this concept. Researchers in different countries observed this shift in marketer's orientation towards customer relationship and started exploring the phenomenon. The initial approachable broadly classified as:

1. The Anglo-Australian Approach.
2. The Nordic Approach, and
3. The North American Approach.

The Anglo-Australian Approach integrated the contemporary theories of quality management, services marketing and customer relationship economics to explain the emergence of relationship marketing. The Nordic Approach views relationship marketing as the confluence of interactive network theory, services marketing and customer relationship economics. The interactive network theory of industrial marketing views the marketing as an interactive process in a context where relationship building is an area of primary concern for marketers. In contrast, the initial focus of the North American scholars was on the relationship between the buyer and seller operating within the context of the organisational environment which facilitated the buyer seller relationship.

ARCHITECTURE OF CRM

The architecture of CRM can be divided into the following three parts:

Operational CRM

This refers to the measures supporting the front office business processes, including customer contact. Tasks resulting from these processes are forwarded to employees responsible for them, while simultaneously, the information necessary for carrying out the tasks' interfaces with back-end applications is provided, and activities involving interactions with customers are documented for further reference.

Analytical CRM

In case of analytical CRM, the data gathered within the operational CRM tasks as well as from other sources are analyzed to segment customers or to identify the potential for enhancing the relationship with the client. Customer analysis can typically lead to targeted campaigns to increase the share of the customer's wallet.

Collaborative CRM

Collaborative CRM facilitates effective interactions with customers through a variety of channels viz., personal, letter, fax, phone, Web, e-mail, etc., and supports the co-ordination between employee teams and channels. This integrates people, processes and data together so that the firms can offer better services to customers and retain them over longer periods.

NEED FOR CRM

The purpose of CRM is not limited to merely improving customer service, it also allows companies to acquire customers and serve them, increase the value of the customer to the organisation, retain good customers and determine which customers can be retained or given a higher level of service.

A good CRM programme can improve customer service by:

(a) Providing product information and technology assistance with an accessibility for 24 hours a day, seven days a week.

(b) Identifying the difference in qualities perceived by different customers and then by designing a suitable service strategy for each customer based on expectation.

(c) Helping to identify potential problems quickly, even before they occur.

(d) Providing a fast mechanism for managing follow-up sales calls to assess post-purchase problems, repurchase probabilities, repurchase times, frequencies, etc.

(e) Providing a fast mechanism for handling problems and complaints, etc.

(f) Using Internet cookies to track customer interests.

(g) Integrating other functional systems and thereby providing accounting and production information to customers when they need it.

Although there are still many grey areas in CRM implementation, an attempt has been made to identify the components of CRM, which is viewed as a major element of present corporate strategy. When CRM is well-understood as a concept, it could be cost effectively implemented with the help of advanced information technologies. Companies need to consider the following issues before implementing CRM:

- Nature of core business
- Future prosperity of the business
- Appropriate form of CRM needed

- Suitable information technology (IT) infrastructure needs.

As organisations become more sophisticated, they need to creatively integrate technologies to support the relevant CRM strategies for mapping out their businesses. The CRM attracts greater focus and will have to be able to reach a much more sophisticated level of one-to-one management and data mining.

FEATURES OF A GOOD CRM PROGRAMME

A good CRM programme of the firm can improve its customer service by facilitating communication in the following ways:

(a) Offering product information, product usage information and technical support through the web and other means round the clock.

(b) Offering services in keeping with the requirements and expectations of each individual customer.

(c) Providing a speedy mechanism for the purpose of managing and scheduling follow-up sales and calls in order to analyze the post-purchase cognitive dissonance, the probabilities of re-purchase, number of times of re-purchases and frequency of repurchases.

(d) Developing an effective system to track all possible points of contact between the firm and the customer in an integrated manner.

(e) Locating the potential problems well in advance even before such problems arise.

(f) Facilitating the adoption of a user-friendly mechanism for registering the complaints from the customers to prevent customer dissatisfaction.

(g) Suggesting a speedy mechanism for correcting service deficiencies, which may lead to higher customer satisfaction.

(h) Ensuring the maximum utilization of IT-enabled services for offering customers the best and timely services.

(i) Providing a mechanism for improving efficiency and effectiveness in customer service, and for managing and scheduling maintenance, repair, and on-going support.

ROLE OF CRM IN IMPROVING CUSTOMER RELATIONSHIP

The CRM programmes, implemented by firms, help to improve the relationship between the customers and the firm. The effective implementation of CRM results in:

(a) Tracking of customer interests, needs, and buying habits, likes and dislikes, tastes and preferences on a continuous basis and formulation of dynamic marketing strategies. This enables the customers to avail of exactly what they want.

(b) CRM can be employed to micro-segment, the buying centre and can help in industrial market segments.

(c) CRM can be used in improvements of customer service to facilitate long-term sustained customer satisfaction. It thus paves the way for enhanced customer satisfaction, encouraged repeat purchase, improved customer loyalty, reduced customer switchover, economization of marketing costs, and augmentation of the sales revenue, thereby contributing towards a greater profit margin for the firm throughout life.

(d) CRM establishes an in-depth understanding between the firm and its customers, thus enabling the firm to attain a higher rate of repeat purchases.

CRM AND TECHNOLOGY

CRM is a primarily centre on customers. Organisations planning CRM projects begin with the premise of giving customers the attention and service they expect from the organisation and in fact more, and then think in terms of which technology can help in achieving this purpose. In theory one can implement CRM without any technology but not in practice, if the customer strength crosses a few dozens. But technology is a vehicle and a means to an end. Technology is not an end in itself. Today's Internet, Communications and Information Technologies help organisations to establish one to one relationship with thousands and even millions of customers, spread across the globe. These technologies have become essential enablers of CRM in the present form. Due to this factor, many people especially software vendors try to equate CRM with technology. Nothing can be far from the truth. Technology is a tool, a very important tool, but certainly not CRM by itself.

GOALS OF CRM

The CRM is an organisational strategy to develop mutually profitable lifelong relationship with the customer. The goals of CRM are to:

- Use technology and human resources to understand the needs and behaviour of present and potential customers;
- Acquire, retain and establish mutually rewarding one to one relationships with customers;
- Provide better customer service to customers;
- Identify high value customers so that the organisation can serve them better with differential service;
- Collect customer information at all possible points and making this information available to the entire organisation wherever and whenever needed, so that the customer could be served better;
- Get maximum 'wallet share' of the customer;

- Increase customer revenues by cross selling and up selling;
- Simplify marketing and sales processes;
- Provide the level of service required to be provided to high value customers;
- Integrate all customer related activities like marketing, sales, service in such a way that the highest value is provided to the customer.

Internet provided an opportunity for more interactions between the organisations and customers and businesses also found a number of opportunities for customer acquisition and retention. Businesses felt that by developing unified view of the customers across the enterprise, they could better understand and serve the customer, increase the customer retention which in turn will increase their profits.

The CRM strategies assist organisations as they work to identify, satisfy, retain, and maximize the value of their best customers. Inherent in these strategies is the notion that business and marketing activities need to focus on increasing customer life-time value. Customer life-time value can be described as the discounted net profit a business or organisation makes from a customer, and may be estimated by considering a customer's purchase and promotional histories, as well as shopping preferences.

ADVANTAGES OF CRM

CRM facilitates the following:

(i) Speed and accuracy in information analysis

(ii) Better understanding of customer behaviour

(iii) Business process re-engineering.

(iv) Customers usage pattern

(v) New product development

(vi) Central data management

(vii) Retention of Customers after sales service

(viii) Improve cross-selling and up-selling

(ix) Improve the effectiveness of field service

(x) Identify and target the best customers and generation of quality leads for the sales force

(xi) Make management of marketing and sales campaigns more effective by setting well-defined goals

(xii) Understand the needs of employees and maintain a sound relationship with them.

(xiii) Reduction in Advertising costs

(xiv) Allows organisations to compete based on services and not prices and

(xv) Provision of single point contact with a customer.

At the macro level there was an economic downturn during 2001 and 2002. During economic down turn it is quite natural for the enterprises to tighten their belts by resorting to cost cutting measures. Many decided to postpone their high dollar value expenditures and projects like CRM. It so happened that the timing of expected results from the CRM projects coincided with this downturn and consequent decisions. Putting two and two together critics like Arthur O'Connor prematurely wrote the obituary of CRM.

STEPS FOR SUCCESSFUL CRM

The following steps would ensure the successful implementation of CRM in any firm:

❖ Managers should only think about providing quality customer services rather than concentrating more on the CRM label. The success lies in implementation of CRM and not in following vague policies.

- In order to understand the specific CRM needs, the firm has to re-examine the vital CRM areas like strategy, communication, software tools, etc.
- The effective implementation of CRM necessitates the availability and allocation of adequate funds.
- CRM implementation can be undertaken on a small scale in the initial stages, which will help the firm find out the pitfalls and practical difficulties. This would help the firm to adopt the required corrective measures at the time of the full-fledged implementation of CRM.
- The firms should focus on the CRM integration and data mining.
- Instead of abandoning the existing systems and data, the firm must retain them when introducing new CRM strategies.
- The firm must carry out proper periodical evaluation to measure the success of its CRM strategy.
- The firm must wait for the right opportunity to reap benefits arising out of the implementation of new CRM strategies.
- The motto of the CRM strategy of the firm should be to enhance the sharing of the information between the firm and its customers for maintaining a long-term sustained relationship. This would enable the firm to deliver better services to the customers.

The effective implementation of CRM strategies thus allows a firm both to retain the existing customers as well as to attract new customers. By adopting a CRM system, the firm can keep track of various basic and vital customer information such as contacts, communications, accounts, buying histories and preferences. Through proper maintenance of data relating to the customers, the firm can improve contacts with its customers, manage marketing campaigns, reduce customer response times and offer services in a large and geographically widely spread out market.

CONCEPTS USED IN THE STUDY

Concepts used in the study are presented below:

Consumer

Consumer is defined as an individual who purchases and uses goods or services.

Consumer is defined as someone who buys goods in a personal capacity from a business seller.

Customer

As per chamber's 21st Century Dictionary 'Customer' is 'someone who purchases goods from a shop or uses the services of a business, etc'.

According to the American Marketing Association, "A customer is the actual or prospective purchaser of products or services." The most important asset of any organisation is its customers. A customer is someone who makes use of or receives the products or services of an individual or organisation. An organisation's success depends on how many customers it has, how much they buy and how often they buy.

Customer is a person or an organisation paying money in exchange for goods or services.

Needs

Customer needs may be defined as the goods or services a customer requires to achieve specific goals.

Palmer (2004) defines need as a perceived state of deprivation, which motivates an individual to take action to eliminate that sense of deprivation.[5]

Product

A product is anything that can be offered to a market that might satisfy a want or need. However, it is much more than just a physical object. It is the complete bundle of benefits or satisfactions that buyers perceive they will obtain if they purchase the product. It is the sum of all physical, psychological, symbolic, and service attributes.

Product is a term used to describe all goods and services sold. Products are bundles of attributes (features, functions, and uses) and can be either tangible as in the case of physical goods, or intangibles such as those associated with service benefits or a combination of the two.

Service

Service refers to the identifiable, but sometimes intangible, activities undertaken by a retailer in conjunction with the basic goods and services it sells.

Service is a primary activity associated with after-sale support to enhance or to maintain the value of the product or service.

Expectations

Expectations may be pre-defined, in which case asking customers to state expectations might help formulate or even create them. An assumption that can be made rather confidently is that the act of stating expectations for a service or product experience just before the service encounter or consumption experience makes the stated expectations more accessible and salient during that experience and possibly the subsequent experiences.

Awareness

Saxena (2002) defines awareness as a continuous range from an uncertain feeling that a product is recognized to a belief that is the only one in the product class.[6]

Perception

Perception is as how one gathers and interprets information from the world around us. Perception is the process of acquiring, interpreting, selecting, and organizing sensory information. The word perception comes from the Latin percepio, meaning "receiving, collecting, and action of taking possession, apprehension with the mind or senses."

Preferences

Preferring, i.e. choosing as more desirable; something that is superior to another item or items.

Customer Satisfaction

The word satisfaction is derived from the Latin word 'Satis' and the Latin word ending 'faction' (to do/make). Early usage centred on satisfaction being some sort of release from wrong doing. Later the word came to refer to "release from uncertainty". Modern usage of the word has tended to be much broader and satisfaction is clearly related to other words such as satisfactory (adequate), satisfy (make pleased or contented) and satisfaction (enough).

The American Marketing Association defines customer satisfaction as "the degree to which there is match between the customer's expectation of the product and the actual performance." Expectations are formed based on information consumers receive from sales person, friends, family, opinion leaders, etc. as well as past experience with the product. This is an important measure of the ability of a firm to successfully meet the needs of its customers. The Chamber's 21st Century Dictionary defines satisfaction as "the act of satisfying or the state of feeling of being satisfied."

Satisfaction evolves as a consequence of one party's experience with others ability to fulfil norms and expectations.[7].

Satisfaction is a concept that entails both a cognitive and an effective dimension; it is relative in nature, since it stems mainly from a process of comparison between customer's subjective experience and a reference standard. Satisfaction is linked to post purchase behaviour, and it is impossible to express the satisfaction judgment if the product or service has not been consumed. For customers, satisfaction is a positive feeling, a positive answer to an expectation, or exceeding the expectations.[8] For customers, satisfaction is also related to specific service attributes: contact personnel, competence, friendliness, level of personalization and security.

There are many possible ways to satisfy the needs of target customers. A product might have many different features. Customer service levels before or after the sale can be adjusted. The package, brand name and warranty can be changed. Various advertising media-news papers, magazines, cable and internet may be used. The price can be changed, discounts can be given and so on. With so many possible variables, is there any way or is it possible to organize all these decisions and simplify the selection of marketing mixes to four basic ones, (4Ps) Viz., Product, Price, Place and Promotion.

Product

The Product area is concerned with deploying the light "product" for the target market. This offering may involve a physical good, a service or a blend of both. We are more concerned about the services offered by the FMCG (Fast Moving Consumer Goods) Retailers of Erode district.

Price

Price setting must consider the kind of competition in the target market and the cost of the whole marketing mix. Price is the main source of revenue for an organisation and it is the rate at which the customer purchases the product or uses the services offered. We are more concerned about how the FMCG retailers fix up their customers' pricing during offers, free gifts and other occasions.

Place

Place is concerned with all the decisions involved in getting the product to the target market's place. A product is not much good to a customer if it is not available when and where it is waned. A product reaches customers through a channel of distribution. A channel of distribution is any service of firms that participate in the flow of products from producer to final user or consumer. We are concerned about how the Fast Moving Goods retailers manage their distribution outlets attractively and provide good experience for the customers at the point of purchase and also how they manage their customers effectively.

Promotion

Promotion is concerned with telling the target market or others in the channel of distribution about the product or service. We are concerned about how the retailers promote their product or service in their market area.

There are two distinct types of customers. Customers are external and internal. An external customer can be defined in many ways, such as the one who uses the product or service, the one who purchases the product or service, or the one who influences the sale of the product or service. An external customer exists outside the organisation and generally falls into three categories: current, prospective and lost customers. Performance must be continually improved in order to retain existing customers and to gain new ones. The external customers for this study are the existing users of different Fast Moving Consumer Goods.

Customer Loyalty

Loyal customers are addressed by different names by different organisations like premium customers, key accounts, elites, crown jewels. The term customer loyalty means commitment or attachment to a product, brand, and a store based on favourable attitudes and is reflected by repeat purchases or recommendations to others.

Richard L Oliver defines loyalty as:

"a deeply held commitment to re-buy or re-patronize a perfect product or service consistently in future despite situational influences and marketing efforts having the potential to cause switching behaviour."

The suggested metric for the brand loyalty can be given as follows.

Brand Loyalty = Number of times a particular brand product is purchased/total number of similar product purchases

Customer Retention

Customers have become very fickle now. With the cost of acquiring new customers is on the ascendance, retention of customers is very important for business success. In a widely published study Frederick Reichheld (1996) found that every five years, US companies are losing more than 50% of their customers. With the data analysis tools that are available, CRM vendors are offering very sophisticated churn prediction products that can help in planning churn prevention strategies by identifying the customers that are likely to leave by comparing like attributes of customers and plan suitable retention strategies.

Use of Preferred Channels

Different customers prefer different channels of communication. Some like to be contacted by email whereas some others might like to be contacted personally. CRM tools help organisations in understanding individual customer's channel preferences and contact them using their preferred means. Studies indicate personalized messages on preferred channel result in a high response rate for the marketing programmes.

Retailing

Retailing consists of the sale of goods or merchandise from a fixed location such as a department store or kiosk, in small or individual lots for direct consumption by the purchaser. Retailing may include subordinated services, such as delivery. A retailer buys goods or products in large quantities from manufacturers or importers, either directly or through a wholesaler, and then sells smaller quantities to the end-user. Retailers are at the end of the supply chain. Manufacturing marketers see the process of retailing as a necessary part of their overall distribution strategies.

Newman and Cullen define that retailing is the set of activities that market products or services to final consumers for their own personal or household use. It does this by organizing their availability on a relatively large scale and supplies them to customers on a relatively small scale. Researchers define that retailing consists of the final activities and steps to place a product in the hands of the ultimate consumer or to provide services to the consumer.

The term "retailer" is also applied where a service provider services the needs of a large number of individuals, such as a public utility like electric power. Shops may be on residential streets, shopping streets with few or no houses or in a shopping mall. Sometimes a shopping street has a partial or full roof to protect customers from precipitation. Online retailing, a type of electronic commerce used for business-to-consumer (B2C) transactions and mail order, are forms of non-shop retailing.

Retailing in India

The retailing industry has been present in our country through history and is considered as one of the largest sectors in the Indian economy, contributing to around 14 per cent to the GDP, and employing around 7% of the total population. For decades, retailing in India has been highly fragmented, i.e., unorganized, due to the presence of huge number of small mom-n-pop stores. While retailing industry has been present for centuries, it is only in the recent times that it has witnessed so much dynamism and corporate attention. It is the latest bandwagon that has witnessed hordes of big players like TATA, Birla, Reliance, Pantaloon Group, etc. leaping into it. The entry of big players in retailing has caused a major revolution in its marketing strategies and innovations. Now retail sector, being considered as the most dynamic and attractive sector in India, is going through a transition phase. (*See Table 3.1 on next page*)

India is a unique country. Companies cannot have readymade formats for this market. It is said that the consumer taste and preference in India changes in every 3 km. of distance. Given the wide cultural difference and diversity, a company cannot follow a format which was popular and successful in a foreign market in India. Company like Wall-Mart successful in U.S.A. was not able to replicate the same story in China and South Korea. Hence the corporates involved in the retail business are cautious in their choice of formats. In fact, companies do not have a specific format. They want to experiment various formats and depending on the success of these formats, they will retain the format for their future expansion.

INDUSTRY STATUS FOR RETAILING

The retail industry is need of huge investment in terms of importing the technology, improving the skills of the workforce and other sorts of investments. According to FICCI, 92 per cent of investments in retailing are made in urban areas where the cost of the real estate is higher. Industry status for retailing will ensure organized flow of funds to the industry augur in its growth.

Unorganized retailing should be organized and store should be designed well and organized to attract the ultimate players like Wall-Mart. Indian retailers must adopt discount stores along with regular format of stores and retailers would develop shopping as entertaining experiences like Tesco, and McDonald's food chain networks.

The entry of foreign players, if allowed, will not only affect ownership, but also change the basics of business. Huge investments in stores and their supply chains can

Table 3.1: Different Formats in Retailing

Format	Description	Advantage	Example
1	2	3	4
Branded Stores	Exclusive showrooms either owned or franchised out by a manufacturer	Complete range available for a given brand, certified product quality	Bharati-wall Mart
Specialty Stores	Focus on a specific consumer need, carry most of the brands available	Greater choice to the consumer, comparison between brands is possible	Health and Glow
Department Stores	Large stores having a wide variety of products, organized into different departments such as clothing, house wares, furniture, appliances, toys, etc.	One stop shop catering to varied/ consumer needs.	Shopper's Stop
Supermarkets	Extremely large self-service retail outlets	One stop shop catering to varied consumer needs	Food World,
Discount Stores	Stores offering discounts on the retail price through selling high volumes and reaping economies of scale	Low Prices	Subhiksha

(Contd…)

1	2	3	4
Hyper-mart	Larger than a supermarket, sometimes with a warehouse appearance, generally located in quieter parts of the city	Low prices, vast choice available including services such as cafeterias.	Spencer's, Big Bazaar, Star India Bazaar.
Convenience stores	Small self-service formats located in crowded urban areas.	Convenient location and extended operating hours.	Reliance Fresh.
Specialty Stores	Focus on a specific consumer need, carry most of the brands available	Greater choice to the consumer, comparison between brands is possible	Departmental Stores

transform the entire scenario. But the lifting of ban is a policy issue that cannot be predicted, and can only be decided by the government and supply chains and logistics network with investments in information technology enabling process effectiveness. Increased volumes would enable investments in specialized equipment for transportation of goods. Retailers with large chains would negotiate and get central procurement but local dispatches from their suppliers.

Time-stressed consumers will also ask for round-the-clock retailing. As these consumers will be ready to pay a premium for service at odd hours, the timings of shopping will have to adapt to the needs of these consumers. A number of 24-hour retail stores should emerge to cater to this particular need. The assumption here is that the current administrative restrictions on running shops at night will be lifted. It is expected that in the face of increasing demand from both the consumers and the industry for regulations regarding retailing will be eased. The Indian economy is highly regulated and the most significant regulation is the restriction of foreign ownership (refer Table 3.2). It should not be relaxed to FDI entry in future. So, every retailer is aware and forces them to stay away.

Table 3.2: Percentage Share of Retailing in different Countries

Country	Organised Retailing (%)	Traditional Retailing (%)
Malaysia	50	50
Thailand	50	50
Philippines	35	65
Indonesia	25	75
South Korea	15	85
China	10	90
India	16	84

CRM AND RETAILING

Levy and Weitz, authors of "Retailing Management", define CRM as, "A business philosophy and set of strategies, programmes, and systems that focus on identifying and building loyalty with a retailer's profitable customers." It is based on the business philosophy that all customers are not profitable in the same way and retailers can increase their profitability by building relationships with their better customers. The goal is to develop a base of loyal customers who patronize the retailer frequently.

The CRM is an iterative process that turns customer data into customer loyalty through four sequential activities shown in the CRM Model (Fig. 3.1).

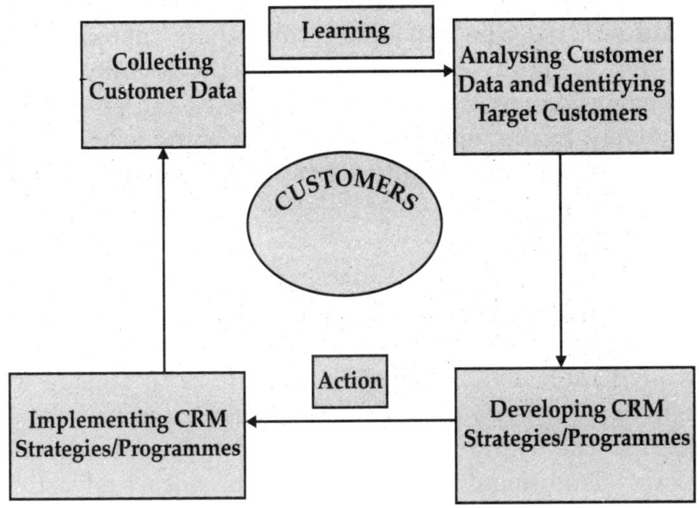

Fig. 3.1: CRM Model

The CRM is quite a new phenomenon in retailing industry. It is only big retailers who have installed CRM systems to identify and track customer purchases and take appropriate management decisions, especially on managing customer relationships. Now, organized retailers like Big Bazaar, Westside, Shoppers' Stop, etc. have started concentrating on providing more value to their valuable customers using targeted promotions and services to increase their share of wallet, i.e., the percentage of the customers' purchases made from these retailers with these customers. Almost all of them have started Loyalty Programmes, i.e., frequent shoppers programme in order to reward the existing customers. These programmes help the retailers in increasing the number of footfalls as well as enhancing their sales revenues and profits. For example, Shoppers' Stop, one of the leading apparel retailer in India, had net sales of Rs. 1.6 Billion, increasing net profits by 96% with the company's loyalty programme, First Citizen Club (a CRM programme) accounting for 63 per cent of the sales.[9]

The organised retailing in India is progressing towards a tough competitive environment where only those retailers would survive who can understand their customers and develop a strong bond with them by developing and implementing appropriate CRM strategies and programmes effectively. In the time to come, CRM is going to be the most dominant marketing tool to enhance the overall retailer performance.

THE CRM AND FMCG

The digital world has opened up a whole new posse of opportunities for organisations with strong brands who sell through intermediaries such as retailers to engage with their most valuable consumers. They can excite them, interest them and inform them in ways unimaginable before. Traditional above the line or broadcast advertising to support the brand and maybe even to drive retail traffic can now be supplemented with real opportunities to engage consumers in the on-line places where they choose to congregate on-line, get to know who they are and then interact with them.

But although this is exciting and can undoubtedly lead to engagement, it is really difficult to measure what impact this has on sales and profit. Traditional direct marketing in Fast Moving Consumer Goods (FMCG) barely breaks even and there have been many that tried (remembering Heinz's forward thinking but failed attempts in the 90s to market across brands using the 'life time value' argument). This economic model is different though and is highly measureable - up to a point.

To manage digital and RM (Relationship Management) interactions in FMCG retailers need to understand the consumers. f mouth, engagement and sales. It is this leadership point that is most challenging for FMCG companies, where the people with the brand power often simply put digital and RM in a box which is marked 'too uncertain and too difficult'. An RM answer to what will get their attention is sales success. RM and Digital champions in FMCG companies have carried out some incredibly innovative attention grabbing campaigns but the sales success is less clear.

REFERENCES

1. Cram, Tony (2001), *Customers that Count,* Financial Times, Prentice-Hall, London, p. 12.
2. Shaw, Robert (2000), *The Foundation for Customer Relationship Management Success*: Enterprise Storage.
3. Starkey and Woodcock (1997), *Journal of the Academy of Marketing Science*, 25(2), pp 139-153.
4. Rigby, R., and Schefter, (2002), Avoid the Four Perils of CRM, *Harvard Business Review*, pp. 101-109.
5. Palmer, Adrian (2004), Introduction to Marketing Theory and Practice, (New Delhi: Oxford University Press), pp. 120-121.
6. Saxena, Rajan (2002), *Marketing Management*, (New Delhi: Tata McGraw Hill), p. 32.
7. Fornell, C. (1992), "A National Customer Satisfaction Barometer the Swedish Experience", *Journal of Marketing*, 56: 6-21.
8. Dano, Florence (2006), Sylvie LLosa, Chiara Orshinger, "Words, Mere Words? An Analysis of Services Customers' Perception of Evaluative Concepts", Quality Management Journal, 13 (2): 46-52.
9. Economic Times, August 12, 2006

An Overview of Fast Moving Consumer Goods (FMCG) *Products and the Retailers Progress*

The organized retail industry in India wants the Union Government to recognize its trade as an 'industry' and make relaxations in foreign direct investment (FDI) norms and formulate policies which improve infrastructure development. Earlier the NDA government had plans to allow 25 per cent FDI in the retail sector in its election manifesto. The Union Government had earlier rejected the proposals of Scojo Foundations Inc of U.S.A., Dover of Switzerland and Eisai of Japan to enter Indian retail sector. Wall-Mart is allowed to set up a subsidiary in India only to outsource and carry out quality checks of goods it out sources from India.

Global Retail Development Index (GRDI) ranks India as the second preferred destination for international retailers, after Russia but ahead of China. While foreign retailers in China are expanding in a big way, in India, the Indian Government is reluctant to allow foreign retailers to open shops. Despite a lower rate of growth of Indian economy compared to China, the scope for organized retailing is much higher in India due to a very small base of the existing organized retailers. At present, India occupies same position in organized retailing as China did about 15 years ago.

At present organized retailing has only 3 per cent share in the total retail market in the country. Over 12 million retail outlets mostly run by small shopkeepers account for 97 per cent of the total retail sales in India. According to a study made by Assocham, 'Retail Scenario in India', the organized retail sector would improve its share to 6 per cent and touch $6 billion now. In 2010, the total retail market in India would grow to $280 billion from $200 billion at present and would account for 7 per cent of India's GDP.

A number of big industrial houses such as Tata, RPG, etc., have also entered the retail business in branded ready-made garments, foods and restaurants, shoes and other FMCG. Retailing is emerging as one of the fastest growing quality employment opportunities in the services sector as retailing houses like Trent Ltd (Westside), Shoppers' Stop. Lifestyle, Globus and a host of brands drive the shift in favour of organized retailing.

In 2005-06, an investment of Rs. 3,000-Rs.4,000 crores was expected to be made in retailing. If the government had allowed FDI, it could have been even more. In June 2005, while Wall-Mart, Tesco and Carrefour were waiting the government to announce FDI in retailing, some Indian companies such as Reliance, Hero, Godrej, Wipro and KK Modi had already decided to foray in retailing. Some existing companies such as the RPG Group, Shopper's Stop and Pantaloon had firmed up plans for expansion of their retail network. Even food retailers such as Pizza Hut and McDonald and garment retailers such as Madura Garments and Arvind Mills were planning to expend. The Hero Group is planning to set up convenience stores in line with US-based '7-Eleven' stores and KK Modi group 'Twenty four Seven' stores modelled on 24-hour grocery stores in the West.

A boom in organized retailing is having a spin-off effect on the construction of malls in India and also organized ancillary industries. In addition to specialized retail storage firms, supply chain management providers and organized retail design companies, demand is also being fuelled from IT hardware and software firms, and manufacturers of air-conditioners, freezer cabinets and microwave ovens from food retailers. In 2005, Wall-mart, Carrefour, Tesco and casino were looking for local partners in India as they were expecting the union government to allow FDI in retailing in 2006, in 2005, while the organized retailing industry in India grew by 30 per cent, the unorganized industry grew by only m7.5 per cent.

In September 2004, the country's leading retailers have formed an association – Retailers association of India – to develop, facilitate and propagate practices and processes that will be good for the growth of the organized retail industry in India. Its founder members comprise Pantaloon Retail (India), Shopper's Stop, Trent, Globus, Piramyd, RPG Retail, Vivek's and Subhiksha. The total size of the retailing industry in India is estimated at around Rs. 10,00,000 crore and the size of the organized retailing industry at 2 per cent of this or Rs. 20,000 crore. The industry is growing at 30-35 per cent annually in the past 5 years. As against this, globally this industry accounts for 10-11 per cent of the GDP.

TYPES OF CONSUMER GOODS

Consumer goods are final goods that are brought from retail stores to satisfy the needs and wants of human being. The consumer goods come in wide variety of product range including household items, personal care products, consumer electronics, utensils, nano-technology devices, foods, clothing products, stationary, gift articles etc. Buying habits of goods by customers such as convenience goods, shopping goods, and speciality goods, durable goods, semi-durable goods, and non-durable goods are increased.

COMMON FMCG RETAIL STORE FORMATS IN INDIA

The following store formats are characterizing the Indian food retailing landscape:

Supermarkets

A supermarket is a store which is more of a large self-service grocery store selling groceries, dairy products and household goods that are consumed regularly. A supermarket format is more prevalent among all modern retail formats in India. These are neighbourhood stores offering home and personal care products and food products that a typical household consumes on a day-to-day basis. These stores are often part of a chain that owns or controls (sometimes by franchise) other supermarkets located in the same or other towns attaining the economies of scale. These stores offer convenience of shopping by making available a large variety of products at one place. Supermarkets usually offer products at low prices by reducing margins. Certain products (typically staples such as bread, milk and sugar) are often sold as loss leaders, that is, with negative margins. To maintain a profit, supermarkets attempt to make up for the low margins with a high overall volume of sales, and with sales of higher-margin items.

Convenience Stores

A convenience store is small store or shop, generally accessible or local. They are often located alongside busy roads, or at gas/petrol stations. This can take the form of gas stations supplementing their income with retail outlets, or convenience stores adding gas to the list of goods on offer. In India few convenience stores like Speedmart, ConveniO's are operated by the oil marketing companies such as IOCL, BPCL and HPCL. Relatively smaller sizes of convenient markets differ from supermarkets.

Discount Stores

Selling merchandise/commodity below the manufacturer's list price is known as discounting. A discount store is a retail store offering a wide range of products, many branded, at discounted prices. A store that sells merchandise, especially consumer goods, at a discount from the manufacturers' suggested retail price. The discount store has become an increasingly popular means of retailing. These discount stores pursue a high-volume, low-profit strategy designed to attract price-conscious consumers. Subhiksha, Marzine Free are some popular discount stores operating in India.

Online Retailing

Though online retailing is popular for merchandising of other consumer durables and services, it is comparatively less intensive in case of food retailing. Few online services (www.fabmall.com/stores/gift) are offering online retailing service for confectionaries (chocolates, cakes and biscuits, sweets, etc). they constitute a very less or no share of food retailing in India since customers generally purchase food items only after seeing and comparing the quality, price etc.

Malls

The malls are the perfect answers for the increasing demand for quality retail space in prime commercial areas that houses a varied segment of large-format retailers and brands, which include food and apparel chains, consumer durables and multiplex operators. As a result, from just three malls in 2000 it has increased to over 220 malls by 2005. The current expected demand for quality retail space in 2006 is estimated to be around 40 million square feet. While previously it was the large, organized retailers – with their modern, up-market outlets, and direct consumer interface-who had been a key factor driving the growth of organized retail in the country, now it is the malls that are playing the role. By 2009, total mall space in the 6 cities of Mumbai, Bangalore, Hyderabad, Chennai, Kolkata, and National Capital Region (Delhi, Noida, Gurgaon) is expected to increase to over 21.1 million sq.ft. Kolkata and Hyderabad are relatively new entrants in the mall segment, but are witnessing quick growth. Smaller cities like Pune,

Ahmedabad, Lucknow, Ludhiana, Jaipur, Chandigarh and Indore, are also expected to see a formidable growth in the growth of malls in the near future.

The importance of understanding the crucial elements of customer relationship management (CRM) becomes increasingly clear when one considers there is no person to person opportunity to form relationships in an e-business. E-business must therefore depend on elements of the customer website interaction to deliver a satisfying relationship. There has been little work on determining and defining exactly what CRM is in the regular business channels (although there has been a lot of talk and guessing) and even less in the e-business channel. Given the possible hundreds of factors that could define CRM on a website, no research indicates which ones are important. So while the goals of CRM are clear, the elements and means to those goals are not. The purpose of this study is to identify the main CRM attributes of e-business.

GLOBAL RETAILING INDUSTRY

The latter half of the 20th century, in both Europe and North America, has seen the emergence of the supermarket as the dominant grocery retail form. The reasons why supermarkets have come to dominate food retailing are not hard to find. The search for convenience in food shopping and consumption, coupled to car ownership, led to the birth of the supermarket. As incomes rose and shoppers sought both convenience and new tastes and stimulation, supermarkets were able to expand the products offered. The invention of the bar code allowed a store to manage thousands of items and their prices and led to 'just-in-time' store replenishment and the ability to carry tens of thousands of individual items. Computer-operated depots and logistical systems integrated store replenishment with consumer demand in a single electronic system. On the Global Retail Stage, little has remained the same over the last decade. One of the few similarities with today is that

Wall-Mart was ranked the top retailer in the world then and it still holds that distinction. Other than Wall-Mart's dominance, there's little about today's environment that looks like the mid-1990s. The global economy has changed, consumer demand has shifted, and retailers' operating systems today are infused with far more technology than was the case six years ago.

The global retail industry has travelled a long way from a small beginning to an industry where the world wide retail sales alone is valued at $ 7 trillion. The top 200 retailers alone account for 30 per cent of worldwide demand. Retail sales being generally driven by people's ability (disposable income) and willingness (consumer confidence) to buy, compliments the fact that the money spent on household consumption worldwide increased 68% between 1980 and 2003. The leader has in-disputably been the USA where some two-thirds or $ 6.6 trillion out of the $ 10 trillion American economy is consumer spending. About 40% of that ($ 3 trillion) is spending on discretionary products and services. Retail turnover in the EU is approximately Euros 2000 billion and the sector average growth looks to be following an upward pattern. The Asian economies (excluding Japan) are expected to grow at 6 per cent consistently till 2007-08. Positive forces at work in retail consumer markets today include high rates of personal expenditures, low interest rates, low unemployment and very low inflation.

Modern Trade – The Organized Retailers

Within modern trade, we have:

1. The discounter (Subhiksha, Apna Bazaar, Margin Free)
2. The value-for-money store (Nilgiris)
3. The experience shop (Foodworld, Trinethra)
4. The home delivery (Fabmart)

Table 4.1: Worlds' Top 10 Retailing Industries

Rank	Country of Origin	Name of Company	Formats	Retail Sales in 2007 (US $ MILLIONS)	Countries of Operation
1	2	3	4	5	6
1.	U.S.	Walmart	Discount, Hypermarket, Supermarket, Superstore, Warehouse	217799	Argentina, Brazil, Canada China, Germany, Mexico, Puerto Rico, S.Korea, UK, US
2	France	Carrefour	Cash & Carry, Convenience, Discount, Hypermarket, Supermarket	61565	Argentina, Belgium, Brazil, Chile, China Columbia, Czech Rep, France, Dominican Repub, Greece, Indonesia, Italy, Japan, Madagascar, Malaysia, Mauritius, Mexico, Morocco, Oman, Poland, Portugal, azarRomania, Singapore, Slovakia, Spain, South Korea, Switzerland, Taiwan, Thailand, Turkey, UAE.
3.	Netherlands	Royal Ahold	Cash & Carry, Discount, Drug	57976	Argentina, Brazil, Chile, Costa Rica, Czech

(Contd...)

1	2	3	4	5	6
4.	U.S.	Home Depot	DIY, Speciality	53553	Canada, Mexico, Puerto Rico, US
5.	U.S.	Kroger	Convenience, Discount, Speciality, Supermarket, Warehouse	50098	US
6.	Germany	Metro AG	Cash & Carry, Department, DIY, Hypermarket, Specialty, Superstore	43357	Austria, Belgium, Bulgaria, China, Croatia, Czech. Rep, Denmark, France, Germany, Greece, Hungary, India, Italy, Japan, Luxembourg, Morocco, Netherlands, Poland, Portugal, Romania, Russia, Slovakia, Spain, Switzerland, Turkey, UK, Ukraine, Vietnam

(Contd...)

1	2	3	4	5	6
7.	U.S.	Target	Department, Discount	49355	U.S.
8.	U.S.	Albertson's	Drug, Supermarket, Warehouse	37931	U.S.
9.	U.S.	Kmart	Discount, Superstore	36151	US
10.	U.S.	Sears	Department, Mail Order, Specialty	35843	Canada, Puerto Rico, U.S.

Source: 2005 Global Retail Report, Deloitte Touche Tohmatsu

While the focus of this note is on modern organized retail trade, we hereunder present insights into the smaller, semi and unorganized retailers.

INTEGRATION OF FMCG INDUSTRY – THE KEY DRIVER OF RETAIL IN INDIA

India is world's second largest grower of fruits and vegetables after Brazil and China. While the agriculture sector has witnessed several leaps of innovation and technological advancements, the processing sector is still in its infancy. Even with less than 4 per cent processing of fruits and vegetables, the Food Processing Industry sector in India is one of the largest in terms of production, consumption within India, export and growth prospects. The government has accorded it a high priority, with a number of fiscal reliefs and incentives, to encourage commercialization and value addition to agricultural produce; for minimizing pre/post harvest wastage, generating employment and export growth. As a result of several policy initiatives undertaken since liberalization in early 90s, the industry has witnessed fast growth in most of the segments. In the following few paragraphs, it can be noted that the processed food market for India is vast and the amount of scope that retail chains would be exposed to is phenomenal taking into consideration the demographics and raise in standards of living. Retailers could throng the market with all these processed and packaged foods with their private labels.

India has also seen a flurry of food chain majors like McDonalds, Pizza Hut and Kentucky Fried Chicken finding their place among the Indian consumers. The trend still follows for food chains in India to spread to almost all cities and towns. These advancements have revolutionized the integration of the Indian Food Industry and has played a vital role in solving, to a large extent, major supply chain issues that prevailed. The trend is that these successful institutional intervention models be replicated and spread in all segments of the food industry far and wide through the country that benefit all the incumbents of the chain evolve. This finally helps the retailer as his supply chain becomes much leaner and vertically integrated. He is in a position to offer a wide variety and highest degree of convenience to his customer.

India's leading FMCG Retailing industries are:

1. Subhiksha
2. Wall-Mart Stores Inc
3. Dish Washing Bars and Powders
4. Hair Care Products
5. Shampoos
6. Toothpastes
7. Fairness Creams
8. Talcum Powders
9. Ajanta India Ltd
10. Anchor Health and Beauty Products Ltd.
11. Cavin Kare Pvt Ltd
12. Collgate-Palmolive
13. Hindustan Uniliver Limited (HUL)
14. Dabur
15. Emami Ltd
16. Godrej Consumer Products Ltd.
17. Indian Household and Healthcare Ltd, etc.

Performance of FMCG

On an average, the prominent players in this retail format have recorded four-fold increase in the number of retail outlets in 2005 and the growth is estimated to be 140 percent in 2010. In terms of retail space, these retailers have expanded nearly six-fold in 2006 as compared to the previous year; signifying that the new outlets are getting much larger in size. Retail sales of these retailers grew nearly 70 per cent in 2005 and more than doubled in 2006.

According to an AC Nielson census of the modern format retail trade, the average FMCG turnover per day is the highest in hyper markets at Rs. 9.7 lakh, followed by departmental stores at Rs. 68,000, discount stores Rs. 30,000, convenience stores Rs. 12,000 and health and pharmacy Rs. 9,000.

RECENT TRENDS AND DEVELOPMENT

The retail sector has been a consumer-led industry. FMCG retail largely depends upon the consumer's ability (purchase power) and consumer's willingness (consumer's confidence).

Increased Use of Technology

The FMCG retailers have been offered with a range of technology applications in recent years. A study indicates that among all the applications, the point-of-sale system continues to be more important, without which business comes to a halt and many other applications cannot function. About 42 per cent of the retailers favour this type of point-of-sale system, as a top priority technology, followed by category management technology applications. The one among the point-of-sale systems is the RFID (Radio Frequency Identification) technology which is widely being used now. The RFID technology aims at reducing the costs, optimizing supply chain processes and improving productivity and profits. Countries such as the U.S., U.K and Japan are leading the way in deploying RFID technology, though China is expected to close the gap by 2009. The RFID technology offers many benefits that include improved efficiency and visibility, lower costs, lower inventory levels yet constant product availability, better asset utilization and increased sales through better out-of-stock goods management. With Wal-mart mandating the use of RFID amongst its top-100 suppliers, and others like Tesco, Metro, JC Penny, Gap and Marks & Spencer joining the RFID bandwagon, the technology is well on its way to establishing a stronghold within the retail sector.

EVOLUTION OF ORGANIZED RETAILING

Retailing, one of the largest sectors in the global economy, is going through a transition phase in India. For a long time, the corner grocery store was the only choice available to the consumer, especially in the urban areas. This is slowly giving way to international formats of retailing. The traditional food and grocery segment has seen the emergence of supermarkets/grocery chains, convenience stores and fast-food chains.

The traditional grocers, by introducing self-service formats as well as value-added services such as credit and home delivery, have tried to redefine themselves. However, the boom in retailing has been confined primarily to the urban markets in the country. Even there, large chunks are yet to feel the impact of organized retailing. There are two primary reasons for this. First, the modern retailer is yet to feel the saturation' effect in the urban market and has, therefore, probably not looked at the other markets as seriously. Second, the modern retailing trend, despite its cost-effectiveness, has come to be identified with lifestyles.

It was only in the year 2000 that the economists put a figure to it: Rs. 400,000 crore (1 crore = 10 million) which is expected to develop to around Rs. 800,000 crore by the year 2005 – an annual increase of 20 per cent. Retailing in India is unorganized with poor supply chain management perspective. According to a recent survey by some of the retail consulting bodies, an overwhelming proportion of the Rs. 400,000 crore retail markets are Unorganized. In fact, only a Rs. 20,000 crore segment of the market is organized. As much as 96 per cent of the five million-plus outlets are smaller than 500 square feet area. This means that India per capita retailing space is about two square feet (compared to 16 square feet in the United States). India's per capita retailing space is thus the lowest in the world.

Currently the retail landscape is filled with Super-market chains with over 1000 outlets all over the country to increase to around 5000 by the 2008. The success of a couple of hyper marts indicates the evolution of hypermarkets in the country prominent among them is Giant, Metro, Big Bazaar models. While the average bill value at a supermarket is in the range of Rs. 300 per bill, the average bill amount at a Hypermarket is in the range of Rs. 750-1000, indicating that the model is in tune with the global models where the average spend is increasing with the shopping experience.

Impact of Technology

The other important aspect of retailing relates to technology. It is widely felt that the key differentiator between the successful and not so successful retailers is primarily in the area of technology. Simultaneously, it will be technology that will help the organized retailer score over the unorganized players, giving both cost and service advantages.

Retailing is a 'technology-intensive' industry. Wal-Mart pioneered the concept of building a competitive advantage through distribution and information systems in the retailing industry. They introduced two innovative logistics techniques - cross-docking and electronic data interchange. Today, online systems link point-of-sales terminals to the main office where detailed analyses on sales by item, classification, stores or vendor are carried out online. 'Data Warehousing' is an established concept in the advanced nations. With the help of 'database retailing', information on existing and potential customers is tracked. Retailing, as discussed before, is at a nascent stage in India. Most organized players have managed to put the front ends in place, but these are relatively easy to copy. The relatively complicated information systems and underlying technologies are in the process of being established. Most grocery retailers such as Food World have started tracking consumer purchases through CRM. The traditional retailers will always continue to exist but organized retailers are working towards revamping their business to obtain strategic advantages at various levels - market, cost, knowledge and customer. With differentiating strategies - value for money, shopping experience, variety, quality, discounts and advanced systems and technology in the back-end, change in the equilibrium with manufacturers and a thorough understanding of the consumer behaviour, the ground is all set for the organized retailers.

Table 4.2: Year of Establishment of Retailers

Sl. No.	Year	No. of Respondents	Per cent
1.	Below 6 years	97	19.0
2.	6-10 years	225	44.1
3.	11-15 years	133	26.1
4.	Above 15 years	55	10.8
	Total	**510**	**100.0**

RETAILER PROGRESS ON FMC PRODUCTS

Year of Establishment of Relatives

It could be noted from Table 4.2 that 19 per cent of the retailers have established their retail shops for less than six years, 44.1 per cent of the retailers have established their retail shop for 6-10 years, 26.1 per cent of the retailers have established their retail shop for 11-15 years and remaining 10.8 per cent of the retailers established their retail shop for more than 15 years. It is concluded from the table that majority of the respondents have established their retail shop for 6-10 years.

Table 4.3: Experience of the Retailers

Sl. No.	Experience	No. of Respondents	Per cent
1.	1-3 years	94	18.4
2.	4-6 years	113	22.2
3.	7-9 years	203	39.8
4.	10 years and above	100	19.6
	Total	**510**	**100.0**

EXPERIENCE OF THE RELATIVES

It is clear from the Table 4.3 that 18.4 per cent of the retailers have 1 to 3 years of experience, 22.2 per cent of the retailers have 4 to 6 years of experience, 39.8 per cent of the retailers have 7 to 9 years of experience and the remaining 19.6 per cent of the retailers have 10 years of experience. It is concluded that majority of the respondents have 7 to 9 years of experience.

Table 4.4: Number of Retail Outlets

Sl. No.	No. of retail outlets	No. of Respondents	Per cent
1.	1	279	54.7
2.	2	83	16.3
3.	3	52	10.2
4.	4 and above	96	15.8
	Total	**510**	**100**

NUMBER OF RETAIL OUTLETS

It is pin-pointed from Table 4.4 that 54.7 per cent of the retailers have only one retail outlet, 16.3 per cent of the retailers have two retail outlets, 10.2 per cent of the retailers have three retail outlets and remaining 15.8 per cent of the retailers have four retail outlets. It is concluded from the table that majority of the respondents have only one retail outlet.

Table 4.5: Opinion on the given Factors of Customers While Purchasing the Goods

Sl. No.	Factors	Respondents Opinion			WA*	Rank
		Good	Moderate	Poor		
1.	Customers Expectations	428	72	10	340	I
2.	Customers Attitude	268	222	20	211	III
3.	Customers Queries	248	154	108	193	V
4.	Customer Perception	258	210	42	206	IV
5.	Customers Knowledge on Selecting the Products	307	175	28	217	II

* WA: Weighted Average.

OPINION ON THE GIVEN FACTOR OF CUSTOMERS WHILE PURCHASING THE GOODS

It is divulged from the Table 4.5 that Majority of the retailers opined about Customers Expectations are good which stands at first rank. Following that customers knowledge on selecting the products are also found good with the weighted score of 217 ranked at second. Retailers give third rank to the Customers attitude towards the products. And the retailers gave Moderate opinion on Customer Perception and Customers Queries which stand fourth and fifth ranks. It is concluded from the above analysis that majority of the respondents opined that the customers' expectations are good.

RELATIONSHIP WITH CUSTOMERS

It is observed from the Table 4.6 (*See on next page*) that 35.3 per cent of the retailers opined that the customers relationship with them is excellent, 42.2 per cent of the retailers opined that the customers relationship with them is good, 22.5 per cent of the retailers opined that the customers relationship with them is medium. It is concluded that majority of the respondents opined that the customers relationship with them is good.

Table 4.6: Relationship with Customers

Sl. No.	Opinion	No. of Respondents	Per cent
1.	Excellent	180	35.3
2.	Good	215	42.2
3.	Medium	115	22.5
4.	Poor	0	0.0
5.	Very Poor	0	0.0
	Total	**510**	**100.0**

TYPE OF PRODUCTS PURCHASED BY CUSTOMERS

It is noted from the Table 4.7 (*See on next page*) that 43.1 per cent of the retailers opined that the customers buy low priced products, 28.0 per cent of the retailers opined that the customers buy rich quality products, 20.8 per cent of the retailers opined that the customers buy more quantity of products, 8.0 per cent of the retailers are opined that the customers' buy products based on advertisements. It is concluded that majority of the respondents opined that the customers buy low priced products.

RETAILERS OPINION ON THE FACTORS OF PURCHASING

It is noted from the Table 4.8 (*See on next page*) that most of the retailers opined that Customer Behaviour is very good while selecting the products in the shop. More number of retailers opined about Customer relationship with salesmen and Customers queries are very good. Few retailers opined that the customers repurchasing behaviour good. And very retailers opined that dealing of customers complaints are not good which is ranked at five. It is, therefore, concluded from Table 4.8 most of the retailers opined that Customer Behaviour is very good while selecting the products in the retail store.

Table 4.7: Type of Products Purchased by the Customers

Sl. No.	Opinion	No. of Respondents	Per cent
1.	Buy Low priced Products	220	43.1
2.	Buy rich quality products	143	28.0
3.	Buy more quantity of products	106	20.8
4.	Concentrate on Advertised products	41	8.0
5.	Buy retailers recommended products	0	0.0
	Total	**510**	**100.0**

Table 4.8: Retailers Opinion on the Factors of Purchasing

Sl. No.	Factors	Respondents Opinion					WA*	Rank
		Very Good	Good	Medium	Poor	Very Poor		
1.	Customer Behaviour	290	127	93	0	0	149	I
2.	Customer relationship with Salesmen	237	180	60	33	0	143	II
3.	Queries by Customers	242	152	78	25	13	141	III
4.	Deal on Customers Complaints	163	94	94	118	41	117	V
5.	Post Purchasing Behaviour of the Customer	160	172	97	34	47	126	IV

* WA – Weighted Average

Role of FMCG Retailers in Practising of CRM and the Problems Faced by them in the Study Area

In this chapter, role of retailers in practicing customer relationship management and the problems faced by them are expressed through data collection. Various statistical tools were used to measure the different variables used in data collection.

Problems Faced by the Retailers with Customers

It is noted from the Table 5.1 that 27.6 percentage of the retailers faced problems with customers and the remaining 72.4 percentage of the retailers did not face any problem with customers. It is concluded that majority of the respondents did not face any problem with customers.

Table 5.1: Problems Faced by the Retailers with Customers

Sl. No.	Opinion	No. of Respondents	Percentage
1.	Yes	141	27.6
2.	No	369	72.4
	Total	**510**	**100.0**

customers' Awareness of New Products

It is observed from the Table 5.2 that 49.0 per cent of the retailers' awareness level is good for new products, 48.8 per cent of the retailers' awareness level is medium for new products and the remaining 2.2 per cent of the retailers' awareness level is poor for new products. It is concluded that majority of the respondents' awareness level is good for new products.

Table 5.2: Customers Awareness of New Products

Sl. No.	Opinion	No. of Respondents	Per cent
1.	Good	250	49.0
2.	Medium	249	48.8
3.	Poor	11	2.2
	Total	**510**	**100.0**

Retailers' Opinion on Training to Customers

It is observed from Table 5.3 that 35.9 per cent of the retailers gave any training to their customers and 64.1 per cent of the retailers did not give any training to their customers. It is concluded that majority of the respondents did not give any training to their customers.

Table 5.3: Retailers' Opinion on Training to Customers

Sl. No.	Opinion	No. of Respondents	Percentage
1.	Yes	183	35.9
2.	No	327	64.1
	Total	**510**	**100.0**

Retailers' Opinion on Training Feedback

It is observed from Table 5.4 that 48.6 per cent of the respondents fully grasped the training, 29.5 per cent of the respondents somewhat grasped the training and the remaining 21.9 per cent of the respondents did not fully grasp the training. It is concluded that majority of the respondents fully grasped the training.

Table 5.4: Retailers' Opinion on Training Feedback

Sl. No.	Opinion	No. of Respondents	Percentage
1.	Fully grasped	89	48.6
2.	Somewhat grasped	54	29.5
3.	Fully not grasped	40	21.9
	Total	**183**	**100.0**

Customer Behaviour with the Retailers

It is identified from the Table 5.5 that 54.9 per cent of the retailers find customer behaviour good and 45.1 per cent of the retailers find customer behaviour as medium. It is concluded that majority of the respondents find customer behaviour good.

Table 5.5: Customer Behaviour with the Retailers

Sl. No.	Opinion •	No. of Respondents	Percentage
1.	Good	280	54.9
2.	Medium	230	45.1
3.	Poor	0	0.0
	Total	**510**	**100.0**

Purchasing Pattern of the Customers

It is observed from Table 5.6 that 34.1 per cent of the respondents opined customers purchase daily, 52.7 per cent of the retailers opined that some customers purchase weekly once, 2.5 per cent of the retailers opined some customers purchase monthly once and 10.6 per cent of the respondents opined some customers purchase monthly twice. It is concluded that majority of the respondents opined the customers are purchase weekly once.

Table 5.6: Purchasing Pattern of the Customers

Sl. No.	Opinion	No. of Respondents	Percentage
1.	Daily	174	34.1
2.	Weekly once	269	52.7
3.	Monthly once	13	2.5
4.	Monthly twice	54	10.6
5.	Other method	0	0.0
	Total	**510**	**100.0**

Mode of Purchase

It is analyzed from Table 5.7 that 82.2 per cent of the retailers opined customers purchase products by cash mode and 17.8 per cent of the retailers opined that customers purchase products by credit mode. It is concluded that majority of the respondents opined that customers purchase products by cash mode.

Table 5.7: Mode of Purchase

Sl. No.	Opinion	No. of Respondents	Percentage
1.	Cash	419	82.2
2.	Credit	91	17.8
3.	Cheque	0	0.0
	Total	**510**	**100.0**

Credit Period of the Customers

It is observed from Table 5.8 that 34.0 per cent of the retailers provide below one week credit period, 39.5 per cent of the retailers provide below one to two weeks credit period and 26.5 per cent of the retailers provide four to five weeks' credit. It is concluded that majority of the respondents opined that they provide below one to two weeks' of credit.

Table 5.8: Credit Period of the Customers

Sl. No.	Opinion	No. of Respondents	Percentage
1.	Below 1 week	31	34
2.	1-2 weeks	36	39.5
3.	3-4 weeks	0	0
4.	4-5 weeks	24	26.5
	Total	**91**	**100.0**

Payment Term

It is seen from Table 5.9 that 61.8 per cent of the retailers opined that some customers give full payment on their purchased product, 12.7 per cent of the retailers opined that some customers give payment by bargain, 8.2 per cent of the retailers opined that some customers give payment after negotiation, 17.3 per cent of the retailers opined that some customers give payment in instalment. It is concluded that majority of the respondents opined that some customers give full payment of their purchased product.

Table 5.9: Payment Term

Sl. No.	Opinion	No. of Respondents	Per cent
1.	Full payment	315	61.8
2.	Bargaining payment	65	12.7
3.	Negotiable payment	42	8.2
4.	Half payment	0	0.0
5.	Installment payment	88	17.3
	Total	**510**	**100.0**

Retailers' Rate on Customer Awareness

It is noted from the Table 5.10, most of the retailers opined that the customers' awareness on advertisements for products are high. More number of retailers rated the awareness on the price discounts of the products are high. Some of the respondents opined that customer's awareness about seasonal offers and samples is moderate. Few retailers' opinion on awareness of customers' offers at introduction stage and offering free gifts are medium. And some of retailers opined that awareness of free coupons among the customers is very low which was ranked at seven. It is concluded that majority of the retailers opined that the customers' awareness on advertisements for products are high.

Table 5.10: Retailers' Rate on Customer Awareness

Sl. No.	Factors	Respondents Opinion			WA*	Rank
		High	Medium	Low		
1.	Price discounts of the Products	315	182	13	220	II
2.	Free gift	207	165	138	182	VI
3.	Free Coupons	215	225	70	123	VII
4.	Samples	236	159	115	190	IV
5.	Advertisements on the Products	384	111	15	232	I
6.	Seasonal offers	241	185	84	196	III
7.	Offers at introduction stage	160	293	57	187	V

* WA – Weighted Average.

The Retailers' Opinion on Availability of Customers' Expected Products

It is noticed from the Table 5.11 that 98.6 per cent of the retailers opined about their customers feel that their expected products are available in the retail shop and the remaining 1.4 per cent of the retailers opined about their customers feeling that their expected products are not available in the retail shop. It is concluded from the that majority of the respondents opined about their customers feeling that their expected products are available in the retail shop.

Table 5.11: The Retailers' Opinion on Availability of Customers' Expected Products

Sl. No.	Opinion	No. of Respondents	Per cent
1.	Yes	503	98.6
2.	No	7	1.4
	Total	**510**	**100.0**

Customers' Enquiries About Requirements

It is cleared from the Table 5.12 that 85.9 per cent of the retailers opined that their customers enquiry on requirements by direct contact, 7.8 per cent of the retailers opined that their customers enquiry on requirements through phone, 4.1 per cent of the retailers opined that their customers enquiry on requirements through servants and 2.2 per cent of the retailers opined that their customers enquiry on requirements through friends. It is concluded that majority of the respondents opined that their customers enquiry on requirements by direct contact.

Table 5.12: Customers' Enquiries About Requirements

Sl. No.	Opinion	No. of Respondents	Per cent
1.	By direct contact	438	85.9
2.	Through phone	40	7.8
3.	Through servants	21	4.1
4.	Through sales representatives	0	0.0
5.	Through friends	11	2.2
	Total	**510**	**100.0**

Advertisements' Support on Customers Preference of Products

It is analyzed from the Table 5.13 that 81.8 per cent of the retailers opined that the advertisement support their customers to prefer the required products and the remaining 18.2 per cent of the retailers opined that the advertisement does not support their customers to prefer the required products. It is concluded that majority of the respondents are felt that the advertisements support their customers to prefer the required products.

Table 5.13: Advertisements' Support on Customers Preference of Products

Sl. No.	Opinion	No. of Respondents	Per cent
1.	Yes	417	81.8
2.	No	93	18.2
	Total	**510**	**100.0**

Media's Influence for Advertisement

It is evident from Table 5.14 (*See on next page*) that 39.1 per cent of the retailers opined that the TV advertisement is most attractive, 5.0 per cent of the retailers opined that the radio advertisement is mostly reached, 15.5 per cent of the retailers opined that the newspaper advertisement is mostly preferred, 37.7 per cent of the retailers opined that the wall banners advertisement is mostly attractive and the remaining 2.7 per cent of the retailers opined that the point of purchase is only preferred. It is concluded that majority of the respondents opined that the wall banners advertisement mostly attracts.

Questions by Customers in the Query Session

It is pinpointed from Table 5.15 (*See on next page*) that 32.9 per cent of the retailers opined that mostly products' usage rate questions will be raised by the customers, 45.7 per cent of the retailers opined that mostly products' life time question will be raised by the customers, 10.4 per cent of the retailers opined that mostly procedures for using products question will be raised by the customers, 1.4 per cent of the retailers opined that mostly new products' availability question will be raised by the customers and remaining 9.6 per cent of the retailers opined that mostly products' discounts or offers will be raised by the customers. It is concluded that majority of the respondents opined that mostly products' life time questions will be raised by the customers.

Table 5.14: Media's Influence for Advertisement

Sl. No.	Opinion	No. of Respondents	Per cent
1.	TV	163	39.1
2.	Radio	21	5.0
3.	Newspaper	65	15.5
4.	Wall banners	157	37.7
5.	Point of purchase	11	2.7
	Total	**417**	**100.0**

Table 5.15: Questions by Customers in the Query Session

Sl. No.	Opinion	No. of Respondents	Per cent
1.	Products' usage rate	168	32.9
2.	Products' life time	233	45.7
3.	Procedure for using products	53	10.4
4.	New products availability	7	1.4
5.	Discounts or offers	49	9.6
	Total	**510**	**100.0**

Hospitality Services in the Shop

It is observed from the Table 5.16 that 12.7 per cent of the respondents feel that they provide hospitality services in their shop and remaining 87.3 per cent of the respondents feel that they do not provide any hospitality services in their shop separately. It is concluded that majority of the respondents opined that the retailers do not provide any hospitality services in their shop separately.

Table 5.16: Hospitality Services in the Shop

Sl. No.	Opinion	No. of Respondents	Per cent
1.	Yes	65	12.7
2.	No	445	87.3
	Total	**510**	**100.0**

Customers' Satisfaction Towards Providing Hospitality Services

It is identified from the Table 5.17 that 75.3 per cent of the retailers opined that their customers are satisfied with their hospitality services and the remaining 24.7 per cent of the respondents opined that their customers are not satisfied with retailers hospitality services. It is concluded that majority of the respondents opined that their customers are satisfied with their hospitality services.

Table 5.17: Customers' Satisfaction Towards Providing Hospitality Services

Sl. No.	Opinion	No. of Respondents	Per cent
1.	Yes	384	75.3
2.	No	126	24.7
	Total	**510**	**100.0**

Maintenance of the Customers DataBase

It is noticed from the Table 5.18 that 57.1 per cent of the retailers maintain customers' details in their database and the remaining 42.9 per cent of the retailers did not maintain their customer database. It is concluded that majority of the respondents maintained their customers details in their data base.

Table 5.18: Maintenance of the Customers Database

Sl. No.	Opinion	No. of Respondents	Per cent
1.	Yes	291	57.1
2.	No	219	42.9
	Total	**510**	**100.0**

Retailers' Opinion on Sending Seasonal Greetings to the Customers

It is observed from the Table 5.19 that 26.9 per cent of the respondents opined that they are sending seasonal greetings to their customers and the remaining 73.1 per cent of the respondents opined that they do not send any seasonal greetings to their customers. It is concluded that majority of the respondents do not send any seasonal greetings to their customers.

Table 5.19: Retailers' Opinion on Sending Seasonal Greetings to the Customers

Sl. No.	Opinion	No. of Respondents	Per cent
1.	Yes	137	26.9
2.	No	373	73.1
	Total	**510**	**100.0**

Type of Greetings Sent by the Retailers

It is identified from the Table 5.20 that 37.2 per cent of the retailers send information about the new products information, 22.7 per cent of the retailers send information about the customers new products information and 40.1 per cent of the retailers send information about the wedding anniversary cards. It is concluded that majority of the respondents send information about the wedding anniversary cards.

Table 5.20: Type of Greetings Sent by the Retailers

Sl. No.	Opinion	No. of Respondents	Per cent
1.	About new products' information	51	37.2
2.	Customers' new products' information	31	22.7
3.	Customers' birthday greetings	0	0.0
4.	Wedding anniversary cards	55	40.1
5.	Discounts and other promotional offer card	0	0.0
6.	Annual details of the company	0	0.0
7.	Others	0	0.0
	Total	**137**	**100.0**

HENRY GARRETT RANKING – ANALYSIS

Types of Customers Purchase in Retail Store

It is clear from Table 5.21 that most of the customers are 'Household People' which ranked first by them with Garrett scores of 35325 points. The second and third places of customers are 'Professionals' and 'Business people' with Garrett scores of 27016 and 26935 points respectively. The fourth and fifth types of customers are 'Employees' and 'Tiny shop owners' with Garrett scores of 25099 and 22192 points respectively. The retailers opined some other type of customers also purchase products ranked as sixth with Garrett scores of 16871 points. It is concluded that the retailers opined most of the customers are 'Household people' and 'Professionals'.

Table 5.21: Types of Customers Purchase in Retail Store

Sl. No.	Type of customers	Total Score	Mean Score	Rank
1.	House Hold People	35325	69.3	I
2.	Business People	26935	52.8	III
3.	Professionals	27016	53.0	II
4.	Employees	25099	49.2	IV
5.	Tiny Shop Owners	22192	43.5	V
6.	Others	16871	33.1	VI

Most Preferred Products by the Customers

Table 5.22 clearly showed the mostly preferred products by the customers in the study area. It could be noted from the analysis that most of the customers preferred to purchase 'Soaps and cosmetics' ranked first by them with Garrett scores of 32558 points. The second and third preferred products are 'Teeth cleaning products' and 'Toiletries' with Garrett scores of 28469 and 27246 points. The fourth and fifth products preferred by the customers are 'Shaving products and detergents' and 'Glassware and light bulbs' with Garrett scores of 26295 and 21949 points respectively. The sixth and seventh ranks occupied by the customers are 'Paper products and Plastic goods' and 'Batteries' with Garrett scores of 21528 and 20148 points. It is concluded that most of the customers preferred to purchase 'Soaps and cosmetics' and 'Teeth cleaning products'.

Table 5.22: Most Preferred Products by the Customers

Sl. No.	Products	Total Score	Mean Score	Rank
1.	Toiletries	27246	53.4	III
2.	Soaps and Cosmetics	32558	63.8	I
3.	Teeth cleaning products	28469	55.8	II
4.	Shaving products and Detergents	26295	51.6	IV
5.	Glassware and Light bulbs	21949	43.0	V
6.	Batteries	20148	39.5	VII
7.	Paper products and Plastic goods	21528	42.2	VI

Reasons for Customers' Preference of the Shop

Table 5.23 (*See on next page*) gives the reasons for the retail shop being preferred by the customers in the study area. It could be observed from the above analysis that most of the customers preferred the retail shop for 'Products availability' with Garret scores of 33487 points respectively. The customers preferred the retail shop for the second and third reasons 'Low price for the Products' and 'Good Service' with Garrett scores of 29755 and 29071 points respectively. The customers preferred the retail shop for the fourth and fifth reasons 'By good relationship' and 'Credit system' with Garrett scores of 22907 and 22656 points respectively. The sixth and seventh reasons are 'Prompt delivery' and 'Near to house' with Garrett scores of 22083 and 18711 points respectively. It is concluded from the above analysis that most of the customers preferred the retail shop for the main reasons of 'Products availability' and 'Low price for the Products'.

Year of Establishment and Level of Satisfaction

It could be observed from the Table 5.24 (*see on next page*) that the level of satisfaction perceived by the respondents with shops established for below five years ranged between 15 and 25 with an average of 19.71. The level of satisfaction perceived by the respondents with establishment for 6-10 years ranged between 11 and 25 with an average of 20.25. Similarly the level of satisfaction perceived by the respondents with those established for 11-15 years ranged between 15 and 24 with an average of 19.19. On the other hand, the level of satisfaction perceived by the respondents where the year of establishment was above 15 years ranged between 17 and 24 with an average of 20.47. From the analysis it is identified that the respondents with those established for above 15 years have the maximum level of satisfaction.

Table 5.23: Reasons for Customers' Preference of the Shop

Sl. No.	Reasons	Total Score	Mean Score	Rank
1.	Products Availability	33487	65.7	I
2.	Low price for the Products	29755	58.3	II
3.	Credit system	22656	44.4	V
4.	Good service	29071	57.0	III
5.	Prompt delivery	22083	43.3	VI
6.	By good relationship	22907	44.9	IV
7.	Near to house	18711	36.7	VII

Table 5.24: Year of Establishment and Level of Satisfaction

Sl. No.	Year	No. of Respondents	%	Average	Range		S.D
					Min	Max	
1.	Below 5 years	97	19.0	19.71	15	25	3.69
2.	6-10 years	225	44.1	20.25	11	25	4.19
3.	11-15 years	133	26.1	19.19	15	24	2.89
4.	Above 15 years	55	10.8	20.47	17	24	2.73
	Total	**510**	**100.0**				

Year of Establishment and Level of Satisfaction (Two-Way Table)

With a view to find the degree of association between the year of establishment and the level of satisfaction, a two-way table was prepared and the result is shown in Table 5.25.

Table 5.25: Year of Establishment and Level of Satisfaction (Two-Way Table)

Sl. No.	Year	Level of Satisfaction			Total
		Low	Medium	High	
1.	Below 5 years	34 (35.1)	28 (28.9)	35 (36.1)	97
2.	6-10 years	69 (30.7)	66 (29.3)	90 (40.0)	225
3.	11-15 years	46 (34.6)	65 (48.9)	22 (16.5)	133
4.	Above 15 years	13 (23.6)	25 (45.5)	17 (30.9)	55
	Total	**162**	**184**	**164**	**510**

Note: Figures in parentheses show percentage.

It is highlighted from the Table 5.25 that the percentage of high level of satisfaction was the highest (40%) among the respondents with those established for 6-10 years and same was the lowest (16.5%) among the respondents with those established for 11-15 years. The percentage of medium level of satisfaction among the respondents was the highest (48.9%) among the respondents established with above 15 years and the same was the lowest (48.9%) among the respondents with those established below 5 years. On the other hand, the percentage of low level of satisfaction was the highest (35.1%) among the respondents with those established for below five years and the same was the lowest (23.6%) among the respondents with those established above fifteen years.

Year of Establishment and Level of Satisfaction (ANOVA)

In order to find the significant difference between the year of establishment and level of satisfaction perceived by the respondents, an ANOVA test was used and the result of the test is shown in Table 5.26.

$H_{0:}$ There is no significant difference between year of establishment and level of satisfaction.

Table 5.26: Year of Establishment and Level of Satisfaction (ANOVA)

Source	SS	DF	MS	F	S
Between Groups	10.942	2	5.471	6.983	Significant at 5% level
Within Groups	397.262	507	0.784		
Total	**408.204**	**509**			

It is witnessed from the above table that the calculated 'F' value is greater than the table value and the result is significant at five per cent level. Hence, the hypothesis, "Level of satisfaction is not influenced by the year of establishment as accepted". From the analysis, it is concluded that there is a significant difference between year of establishment and level of satisfaction.

Retailers Experience and Level of Satisfaction

Table 5.27 suggests that the maximum level of satisfaction perceived by the respondents who have got 1-3 years of experience ranged between 15 and 24 with an average of 19.87. It is followed by 4-6 years experienced respondents' level of satisfaction which ranged between 15 and 24 with an average of 20.30, whereas, satisfaction perceived by the respondents who have got 7-9 years of experience ranged between 11 and 25 with an average of 19.55. The level of satisfaction among the respondents having 10 years and above experience ranged between 17 and 24 with an average of 20.16. Hence, the table reveals that 4-6 years experienced respondents have perceived the maximum level of satisfaction.

Table 5.27: Retailers Experience and Level of Satisfaction

Sl. No.	Experience	No. of Respondents	%	Average	Range		S.D
					Min	Max	
1.	1-3 years	94	18.4	19.87	15	24	3.07
2.	4-6 years	113	22.2	20.30	15	24	3.53
3.	7-9 years	203	39.8	19.55	11	25	4.51
4.	10 years and above	100	19.6	20.16	17	24	2.12
	Total	**510**	**100.0**				

Retailers Experience and Level of Satisfaction (Two-Way Table)

With a view to find the degree of association between experience of the respondents and their level of satisfaction, a two-way table was prepared and the result is shown in Table 5.28. (*See on next page*)

It is identified from Table 5.28 that the percentage of highly level of satisfaction was the highest (46.9%) among the respondents having 4-6 years of experience and the same was the lowest (14%) among the respondents having 10 years and above experience. The percentage of medium level of satisfaction was the highest (63%) among the respondents having above 10 years of experience and the same was the lowest (22.1%) among the respondents having

4-6 years' experience. On the other hand, the percentage of low level of satisfaction was the highest (39.4%) among the respondents having 1-3 years of experience and the lowest (23%) among the 10 years and above experienced respondents.

Table 5.28: Retailers Experience and Level of Satisfaction (Two-Way Table)

Sl. No.	Experience	Level of Satisfaction			Total
		Low	Medium	High	
1.	1-3 years	37 (39.4)	37 (39.4)	20 (21.3)	94
2.	4-6 years	35 (31.0)	25 (22.1)	53 (46.9)	113
3.	7-9 years	67 (33.0)	59 (29.1)	77 (37.9)	203
4.	10 years and above	23 (23.0)	63 (63.0)	14 (14.0)	100
	Total	**162**	**184**	**164**	**510**

Retailers Experience and Level of Satisfaction (ANOVA)

In order to find the significant difference between the experience of the respondents and their level of satisfaction, a ANOVA test was used and the result of the test is shown in Table 5.29.

$H_{0:}$ There is no significant difference between experience of the respondents and their level of satisfaction.

It is understood from Table 5.29 that the calculated 'F' value is greater than the table value and the result is significant at five per cent level. Hence, the hypothesis, "Level of satisfaction is not influenced by the respondent's experience" is accepted. From the analysis, it is concluded that there is a significant difference between experience of the respondents and their level of satisfaction.

Table 5.29: Retailers Experience and Level of Satisfaction (ANOVA)

Source	SS	DF	MS	F	S
Between Groups	49.254	2	24.627	19.771	Significant at 5% level
Within Groups	631.509	507	1.246		
Total	**680.763**	**509**			

Number of Retail Outlets and Level of Satisfaction

It could be seen from Table 5.30 that the level of satisfaction perceived by respondents with only 1 outlet ranged between 15 and 25 with an average of 54.7. It is followed by the respondents having two outlets who perceived the level of job satisfaction that ranged between 17 and 23 with an average of 18.54. The level of satisfaction perceived by the respondents those who have three outlets ranged between 13 and 24 with an average of 17.92. On the other hand, the level of satisfaction perceived by the respondents having 4 and above outlets ranged between 11 and 24 with an average of 15.8. From the analysis, it is identified that the respondents having only 1 outlet perceived the maximum level of satisfaction.

Table 5.30: Number of Retail Outlets and Level of Satisfaction

Sl. No.	No. of Retail Outlets	No. of Respondents	%	Average	Range		S.D
					Min	Max	
1.	1	279	54.7	20.85	15	25	3.36
2.	2	83	16.3	18.54	17	23	1.98
3.	3	52	10.2	17.92	13	24	4.08
4.	4 and above	96	15.8	19.36	11	24	4.51
	Total	**510**	**100.0**				

Number of Retail Outlets and Level of Satisfaction (Two-Way Table)

With a view to find the degree of association between the number of retail outlets and the level of satisfaction, a two-way table was prepared and is shown in Table 5.31.

Table 5.31: Number of Retail Outlets and Level of Satisfaction (Two-Way Table)

Sl. No.	No. of Retail Outlets	Level of Satisfaction			Total
		Low	Medium	High	
1.	1	61 (21.9)	121 (43.4)	97 (34.8)	279
2.	2	41 (49.4)	31 (37.3)	11 (13.3)	83
3.	3	30 (57.7)	12 (23.1)	10 (19.2)	52
4.	4 and above	30 (31.3)	20 (20.8)	46 (47.9)	96
	Total	**162**	**184**	**164**	**510**

Table 5.31 explains that the percentage of higher level of satisfaction perceived by the respondents was the highest (47.9) among the respondents who have 4 and above retails outlets and the same was the lowest (13.3%) among the respondents who have 2 retail outlets. The percentage of medium level of satisfaction perceived by the respondents was the highest (43.4%) among the respondents who have one outlets and the same was the lowest (20.8%) among the respondents who have four and above outlets. On the other hand, the percentage of low level of satisfaction was the highest (57.7%) among the respondents have three retail outlets and the same was the lowest (21.9%) among the respondents who have only one retail outlet.

Number of Retail Outlets and Level of Satisfaction (ANOVA)

In order to find the difference between the experience of the respondents and their level of satisfaction, a chi-square test was used and the result of the test is shown in Table 5.32.

Ho: There is no significant difference between Number of retail outlets and level of satisfaction.

Table 5.32: Number of Retail Outlets and Level of Satisfaction (ANOVA)

Source	SS	DF	MS	F	S
Between Groups	28.817	2	14.408	10.683	Significant at 5% level
Within Groups	683.781	507	1.349		
Total	**712.598**	**509**			

It is clear from Table 5.32 that the calculated 'F' value is greater than the table value and the result is significant at 5% level. Hence, the hypothesis, "Level of satisfaction is not influenced by the number of retail outlets" is accepted. From the analysis, it is concluded that there is a close significant difference between number of retail outlets and level of satisfaction.

Mode of Purchase and Level of Satisfaction

It could be observed from Table 5.33 that the level of satisfaction among the selected sample respondents who purchased by cash mode ranged between 11 and 25 with an average of 19.70. On the other hand, the level of satisfaction among the respondents purchasing by credit mode ranged between 17 and 25 with an average of 20.78. From the analysis it is identified that the maximum level of satisfaction perceived by respondents through credit purchase system.

Table 5.33: Mode of Purchase and Level of Satisfaction

Sl. No.	No. of Retail Outlets	No. of Respondents	%	Average	Range		S.D
					Min	Max	
1.	Cash	419	82.2	19.70	11	25	3.82
2.	Credit	91	17.8	20.78	17	25	2.79
	Total	**510**	**100.0**				

Mode of Purchase and Level of Satisfaction (Two-Way Table)

With a view to find the degree of association between mode of purchase and level of satisfaction, a two-way table was prepared and is shown in Table 5.34.

Table 5.34: Mode of Purchase and Level of Satisfaction (Two-Way Table)

Sl. No.	Mode of Purchase	Level of Satisfaction			Total
		Low	Medium	High	
1.	Cash	140 (33.4)	144 (34.4)	135 (32.2)	419
2.	Credit	22 (24.2)	29 (31.9)	40 (44.0)	91
	Total	**162**	**173**	**175**	**510**

Table 5.34 suggests that the percentage of highest level of satisfaction perceived by the respondents was the highest (44.0%) among the respondents who purchased through credit mode and the same was the lowest (32.2%) among the respondents purchased through cash mode. The percentage of medium level of satisfaction was the highest (34.4%) among the respondents who purchased by cash mode and the same was the lowest (31.9%) among the respondents purchased by credit mode. And the percentage of low level of satisfaction was the highest (33.4%) among the respondents purchased by cash mode and the same was the lowest (24.2%) among the respondents purchased through credit mode.

Mode of Purchase and Level of Satisfaction (ANOVA)

In order to find the difference between the mode of purchase of the respondents and their level of satisfaction, a chi-square (x^2) test was used and the result of the test is shown in Table 5.35.

Ho: There is no significant difference between mode of purchase and level of satisfaction.

Table 5.35: Mode of Purchase and Level of Satisfaction (ANOVA)

Source	SS	DF	MS	F	S
Between Groups	0.574	2	0.287	1.962	No significant at 5% level
Within Groups	74.189	507	0.146		
Total	**74.763**	**509**			

It is explained from the above table that the calculated 'F' value is less than the table value and the result is significant at 5% level. Hence, the hypothesis, "Level of satisfaction is influenced by the mode of purchase" is accepted. From the analysis, it is concluded that there is no significant difference between mode of purchase and level of satisfaction.

Customers' Opinion on CRM Practised by the Retailers of FMCG Products

Age of the Customers

It is clear from Table 6.1 that 34.6 per cent of the respondents belong to below 40 years of age group, 36.1 per cent of the respondents belong to 30-40 years of age group and remaining 29.4 per cent of the respondents belong to above 40 years of age group. It is concluded from the above analysis that majority of the respondents belong to 30-40 years of age group.

Table 6.1: Age of the Customers

Sl. No.	Age	No. of Respondents	Per cent
1.	Below 30 years	394	34.6
2.	30-40 years	411	36.1
3.	Above 40 years	335	29.4
	Total	**1140**	**100.0**

Gender of the Customers

It is observed from Table 6.2, that 44.4 per cent of the respondents are males and remaining 55.6 per cent of the respondents are females. It is concluded from the analysis that majority of the respondents are females.

Table 6.2: Gender of the Customers

Sl. No.	Gender	No. of Respondents	Per cent
1.	Males	506	44.4
2.	Females	634	55.6
	Total	**1140**	**100.0**

Educational Qualifications of the Respondents

It is noted from Table 6.3 that 17.3 per cent of the respondents are educated till school level, 57.5 per cent of the respondents are educated till UG level, 18.2 per cent of the respondents are educated till PG level and remaining 7.0 per cent of the respondents are professionally qualified. It is concluded from the analysis that majority of the respondents are educated up to UG level.

Table 6.3: Educational Qualifications of the Respondents

Sl. No.	Education	No. of Respondents	Per cent
1.	School level	197	17.3
2.	UG	655	57.5
3.	PG	208	18.2
4.	Professional	80	7.0
	Total	**1140**	**100.0**

Occupation of the Respondents

It is clear from Table 6.4 that 5.7 per cent of the respondents are working as government employees, 48.2 per cent of the respondents are engaged in business, 12.5 per cent of the respondents are housewives, 12.0 per cent of the respondents are professionals and 10.8 per cent of the respondents are students and some other group. It is concluded from the analysis that majority of the respondents are engaged in business.

Table 6.4: Occupation of the Respondents

Sl. No.	Occupation	No. of Respondents	Per cent
1.	Govt. Employes	65	5.7
2.	Business	549	48.2
3.	Housewife	143	12.5
4.	Professional	137	12.0
5.	Students	123	10.8
6.	Others	123	10.8
	Total	**1140**	**100.0**

Monthly Income of the Respondents

It is noted from Table 6.5 that 13.2 per cent of the respondents are earning below Rs. 5,000 a month, 45.4 per cent of the respondents are earning from Rs. 5,000 to 10,000 a month, 25.7 per cent of the respondents are earning from Rs. 10,001 to 20,000 a month and the remaining 15.7 per cent of the respondents are earning above Rs. 20,000 a month. It is concluded from the analysis that majority of the respondents are earning between Rs. 5,000-10,000 a month.

Table 6.5: Monthly Income of the Respondents

Sl. No.	Monthly income	No. of Respondents	Per cent
1.	Below Rs. 5,000	150	13.2
2.	Rs. 5,000-10,000	518	45.4
3.	Rs.10,001-20,000	293	25.7
4.	Above Rs. 20,000	179	15.7
	Total	**1140**	**100.0**

Marital Status of the Respondents

It is identified from Table 6.6 that 70.9 per cent of the respondents are married and the remaining 29.1 per cent of the respondents are unmarried. It is concluded from the analysis that majority of the respondents are married.

Table 6.6: Marital Status of the Respondents

Sl. No.	Marital Status	No. of Respondents	Per cent
1.	Married	808	70.9
2.	Un-married	332	29.1
	Total	**1140**	**100.0**

Number of Members in the Family

It is observed from Table 6.7 that 17.8 per cent of the respondents are having below three members in their family, 73.9 per cent of the respondents are having 3 to 6 members in their family and remaining 8.3 per cent of the respondents are having above six members in their family. It is concluded from the analysis that majority of the respondents are having 3 to 6 members in their family.

Table 6.7: Number of Members in the Family

Sl. No.	Number of Family Members	No. of Respondents	Per cent
1.	Below 3 members	203	17.8
2.	3-6 members	842	73.9
3.	Above 6 members	95	8.3
	Total	**1140**	**100.0**

Customers' Relationship with Number of Shops

It is analyzed Table 6.8 that 15.6 per cent of the respondents maintain relationship with one shop, 46.4 per cent of the respondents maintain relationship with two shops, 19.3 per cent of the respondents maintain relationship with three shops and the remaining 18.7 per cent of the respondents maintain relationship with more than three shops. It is concluded from the analysis that majority of the respondents maintain relationship with two shops.

Table 6.8: Customers' Relationship with Number of Shops

Sl. No.	Number of shops	No. of Respondents	Per cent
1.	One	178	15.6
2.	Two	529	46.4
3.	Three	220	19.3
4.	More than three	213	18.7
	Total	**1140**	**100.0**

Period of Awareness of the Retail Shop

It is analyzed from Table 6.9 (*See on next page*) that 9.8 per cent of the respondents are aware about the retail shop for below 3 years, 40.4 per cent of the respondents are aware about the retail shop for 3 to 5 years, 21.1 per cent of the respondents are aware about the retail shop for 6 to 8 years, 1.6 per cent of the respondents are aware about the retail shop for 9 to 11 years and remaining 27.1 per cent of the respondents are aware about the retail shop for above 11 years. It is concluded from the analysis that majority of the respondents are aware about the retail shops for 3 to 5 years.

Source of Awareness About the Retail Shop

It is evident from Table 6.10 (*See on next page*) that 43.4 per cent of the respondents became aware about the retail shop through relatives, 27.5 per cent of the respondents became aware about the retail shop through friends, 14.6 per cent of the respondents have become aware about the retail shop through neighbours, 6.4 per cent of the respondents were aware about the retail shop through offers and advertisement and remaining 8.1 per cent of the respondents became aware about the retail shop through some other sources. It is concluded from the analysis that majority of the respondents became aware about the retail shop through relatives.

Table 6.9: Period of Awareness of the Retail Shop

Sl. No.	Period	No. of Respondents	Per cent
1.	Below 3 years	112	9.8
2.	3-5 years	461	40.4
3.	6-8 years	240	21.1
4.	9-11 years	18	1.6
5.	Above 11 years	309	27.1
	Total	**1140**	**100.0**

Table 6.10: Source of Awareness About the Retail Shop

Sl. No.	Opinion	No. of Respondents	Per cent
1.	Relatives	495	43.4
2.	Friends	313	27.5
3.	Neighbours	167	14.6
4.	Offers and advertisement	73	6.4
5.	Others	92	8.1
	Total	**1140**	**100.0**

Media of Awareness About the Retail Shop

It is divulged from Table 6.11 that 23 per cent of the respondents became aware about the retail shop through television advertisement, 14.0 per cent of the respondents became aware about the retail shop through radio advertisement, 15 per cent of the respondents were aware about the retail shop through newspaper advertisement, 16.5 per cent of the respondents became aware about the retail shop through magazines and remaining 31.5 per cent of the respondents became aware about the retail shop through posters and pamphlets. It is concluded from the analysis that majority of the respondents became aware about the retail shop through posters and pamphlets.

Table 6.11: Media of Awareness About the Retail Shop

Sl. No.	Advertisement	No. of Respondents	Per cent
1.	Television	17	23.0
2.	Radio	10	14.0
3.	Newspaper	11	15.0
4.	Magazines	12	16.5
5.	Posters and Pamphlets	23	31.5
	Total	**73**	**100.0**

Awareness on Other Products Other Than FMCG in Retail Shop

It is identified from Table 6.12 (*see on next page*) that 68.6 per cent of the respondents are aware that the retail shop dealing with some other products not only FMCG products and the remaining 31.4 per cent of the respondents are not aware about these details. It is concluded from the above analysis that majority of the respondents are aware about the retail shop dealing with some other products, not only FMCG products.

Opinion Towards the Retail Shop

It is found from Table 6.13 (*See on next page*), most of the customers opined that the retailers behaviour is very good in the retail shop. More number of customers opined retailers' information on the products is very good while selecting the products. More numbers of customers give third rank for Customers-retailers relations, and some Customers' opinion on Product delivery and quality maintenance stand at fourth and fifth ranks respectively. It is concluded from the analysis that majority of the Customers opined that the Retailers behaviour is very good in the retail shop.

Table 6.12: Awareness on Other Products Other Than FMCG in Retail Shop

Sl. No.	Opinion	No. of Respondents	Per cent
1.	Aware	782	68.6
2.	Not aware	358	31.4
	Total	**1140**	**100.0**

Table 6.13: Opinion Towards the Retail Shop

Sl. No.	Towards Retail Shop	Customers Opinion					WA*	Rank
		Very Good	Good	Medium	Poor	Very Poor		
1.	Retailers behaviour	714	361	65	0	0	347	I
2.	Retailer's information about the product	605	427	108	0	0	337	II
3.	Customer – Retailers relations	578	452	104	6	0	335	III
4.	Product delivery	609	416	36	79	0	332	IV
5.	Quality maintenance	577	377	158	8	20	327	V

* WA – Weighted Average.

Customers' Satisfaction with the Services Offered by the Retail Shops

It is observed from Table 6.14 that 96.7 per cent of the respondents are satisfied with the services offered by the retail shops and the remaining 3.3 per cent of the respondents are not satisfied with the retail shop services. It is concluded from the analysis that majority of the respondents are satisfied with the services offered by the retail shops.

Table 6.14: Customers' Satisfaction with the Services Offered by the Retail Shops

Sl. No.	Opinion	No. of Respondents	Per cent
1.	Satisfied	1102	96.7
2.	Not satisfied	38	3.3
	Total	**1140**	**100.0**

Customers' Satisfaction with Products Availability in the Retail Shop

It is noted from Table 6.15 that 96.5 per cent of the respondents are satisfied with the availability of the products in the retail shops and the remaining 3.5 per cent of the respondents are not satisfied with the availability of the products in the retail shops. It is concluded from the analysis that majority of the respondents are satisfied with the availability of the products in the retail shops.

Table 6.15: Customers' Satisfaction with Products Availability in the Retail Shop

Sl. No.	Opinion	No. of Respondents	Per cent
1.	Yes	1100	96.5
2.	No	40	3.5
	Total	**1140**	**100.0**

Customers Opinion Towards the Services

It is revealed from Table 6.16, most of the Customers opined that the Retailers give very good response towards services provided by them in the retail shop. More number of customers opined that the retailers approach friendly manner to their customers and the delivery systems are very good while purchasing them in the retail stores which stand at second and third ranks respectively. More numbers of customers give fourth rank to Payment system. And the number of customers opined about Bills passing by the retailers is moderate which stands at fifth rank. It is concluded from the analysis that majority of the customers opined that the retailers give very good response towards services provided by them in the retail shop.

Table 6.16: Customers Opinion Towards the Services

Sl. No.	Towards the Services	Customers Opinion					WA*	Rank
		Very Good	Good	Medium	Poor	Very Poor		
1.	Response	777	325	12	26	0	352	I
2.	Friendly approach	605	421	108	6	0	336	II
3.	Payment system	561	396	170	13	0	328	IV
4.	Delivery system	572	468	78	22	0	334	III
5.	Bills passing	613	269	234	16	8	326	V

* WA – Weighted Average.

Customers' Opinion Towards the Products

It is stated from Table 6.17 majority of the customers opined that the product varieties available in the retail shop are very good and which stands at first rank through weighted average score. More number of customers opined that different sizes of the products are also available and the package styles are also very good while selecting them in the retail stores which stand at second and third ranks respectively. More numbers of customers give fourth and fifth ranks for product availability and information about new products. And the number of customers opined about Retailers' information on free products is moderate which stands at sixth rank. It is concluded from the above analysis that majority of the customers opined that the Product varieties available in the retail shop are very good in the retail shop.

Table 6.17: Customers' Opinion Towards the Products

Sl. No.	Towards the Products	Customers Opinion					WA*	Rank
		Very Good	Good	Medium	Poor	Very Poor		
1.	Product varieties	742	393	5	0	0	353	I
2.	Different varieties	674	384	82	0	0	344	II
3.	Package styles	609	376	143	12	0	334	III
4.	Product availability	198	837	81	12	12	308	IV
5.	Information about new products	44	652	360	16	68	267	V
6.	Information about free products	117	206	328	47	442	195	VI

* WA – Weighted Average.

Customers' Opinion Towards the Price-Mix Strategy

It is found from Table 6.18, majority of the Customers opined that price matches with the products through weighted average analysis with the score of 335.3. Most of the customers opined that the price of the products is satisfied in the selected shop which stands at second rank. More numbers of customers give third rank to price discounts for old products. And the number of customers opined about price allowances for new products is moderate which stands at fourth rank. It is concluded from the analysis that majority of the customers opined that price matches with the products in the selected retail shop.

Table 6.18: Customers Opinion Towards the Price-Mix Strategy

Sl. No.	Price-mix Strategies	Customers Opinion					WA*	Rank
		Very Good	Good	Medium	Poor	Very Poor		
1.	Price of the products	615	373	149	3	0	334.7	II
2.	Price matches with products	577	455	108	0	0	335.3	I
3.	Price discounts for old products	581	134	349	76	0	309.0	III
4.	Price allowances for new products	436	312	376	16	0	306.0	IV

* WA – Weighted Average.

Opinion Towards the Promotion Strategy Adopted in the Retail Shop

It is noted from Table 6.19, majority of the customers opined that price discounts are good in the retail shop which stands at first rank with the weighted average score of 836. More number of customers opined that the offers at introduction stage are good with the weighted score of 760 which stands at second rank. More numbers of customers give third and fourth ranks for free gifts to original products and free coupons. And the number of customers opined about Advertisements and Samples given by the retailers and the manufacturers are moderate which stand at fifth and sixth ranks. Also the number of customers stated that seasonal offers given by the retailers are poor stands at seventh rank. It is concluded from the analysis that majority of the customers opined that price discounts are good in the retail store.

Table 6.19: Opinion Towards the Promotion Strategy Adopted in the Retail Shop

Sl. No.	Promotion Strategy	Customers Opinion			WA*	Rank
		Good	Average	Poor		
1.	Price Discounts	836	300	4	519	I
2.	Free Gifts	626	356	155	458	III
3.	Free Coupons	617	368	155	457	IV
4.	Samples	154	852	134	383	VI
5.	Advertisements	623	331	186	453	V
6.	Seasonal Offers	256	562	322	369	VII
7.	Offers at Introduction Stage	760	348	32	501	II

* WA – Weighted Average.

Mode of Purchase

It is observed from Table 6.20 that 99.6 per cent of the respondents purchase products on cash and remaining 0.4 per cent of the respondents purchase products on credit. It is concluded from the analysis that majority of the respondents purchase products in cash.

Table 6.20: Mode of Purchase

Sl. No.	Opinion	No. of Respondents	Per cent
1.	Cash	1136	99.6
2.	Credit	4	0.4
	Total	**1140**	**100.0**

Satisfaction with Present Advertisement

It is noted from Table 6.21 that 67.0 per cent of the respondents are satisfied with the present advertisement and the remaining 33.0 per cent of the respondents are not satisfied with the present advertisement. It is concluded from the analysis that majority of the respondents are satisfied with the present advertisement.

Table 6.21: Satisfaction with Present Advertisement

Sl. No.	Opinion	No. of Respondents	Per cent
1.	Yes	764	67.0
2.	No	376	33.0
	Total	**1140**	**100.0**

Preferable Media for Advertisement

It is analyzed from Table 6.22 that 26.5 per cent of the respondents preferred television as the best media for advertisement, 4.8 per cent of the respondents preferred radio as the best media for advertisement, 30.1 per cent of the respondents preferred newspaper as the best media for advertisement, 23.4 per cent of the respondents preferred magazines as the best media for advertisement, 14.1 per cent of the respondents preferred posters and pamphlets as the best media for advertisement and remaining 1.1 per cent of the respondents preferred some other advertisement media as the best media for advertisement. It is concluded from the analysis that majority of the respondents preferred newspaper media as the best media for advertisement.

Table 6.22: Preferable Media for Advertisement

Sl. No.	Opinion	No. of Respondents	Per cent
1.	Television	100	26.5
2.	Radio	18	4.8
3.	Newspapers	113	30.1
4.	Magazines	88	23.4
5.	Posters and Pamphlets	53	14.1
6.	Others	4	1.1
	Total	**376**	**100.0**

Problems Faced by the Respondents in Utilizing the Service

It is identified from Table 6.23 (*See on next page*) that 65.6 per cent of the respondents faced some problems on utilizing the services offered by the retail shops and remaining 34.4 per cent of the respondents did not face any problems by utilizing the services offered by the retail shops. It is concluded from the analysis that majority of the respondents faced some problems by utilizing the services offered by the retail shops.

Response on Customers Complaints from the Retail Store

It is observed from Table 6.24 (*See on next page*) that 33.4 per cent of the respondents opined as very good for response to the complaints, 35.6 per cent of the respondents opined as good for response of the complaints, 22.1 per cent of the respondents opined as moderate for response of the complaints and 8.9 per cent of the respondents are opined as poor for response of the complaints. It is concluded from the analysis that majority of the respondents opined as good for response of the complaints.

Table 6.23: Problems Faced by the Respondents in Utilizing the Service

Sl. No.	Opinion	No. of Respondents	Per cent
1.	Yes	748	65.6
2.	No	392	34.4
	Total	**1140**	**100.0**

Table 6.24: Response on Customers Complaints from the Retail Store

Sl. No.	Opinion	No. of Respondents	Per cent
1.	Very good	381	33.4
2.	Good	406	35.6
3.	Moderate	252	22.1
4.	Poor	101	8.9
5.	Very poor	0	0.0
	Total	**1140**	**100.0**

Respondents Opinion on Retailers Performance in the Market

It is identified from Table 6.25 that 94.6 per cent of the respondents are satisfied with the retailer's performance in the market and the remaining 5.4 per cent of the respondents are not satisfied with the retailer's performance. It is concluded from the analysis that majority of the respondents are satisfied with the retailer's performance in the market.

Table 6.25: Respondents Opinion on Retailers Performance in the Market

Sl. No.	Opinion	No. of Respondents	Per cent
1.	Satisfied	1078	94.6
2.	Not satisfied	62	5.4
	Total	**1140**	**100.0**

Respondents' Feeling About Expectations are Filled by the Retailers

It is noted from Table 6.26 that 76.7 per cent of the respondents felt that their expectations were filled by the retailers and remaining 23.3 per cent of the respondents felt that their expectations were not filled by the retailers. It is concluded from the analysis that majority of the respondents felt that their expectations were filled by the retailers.

Table 6.26: Respondents' Feeling About Expectations are Filled by the Retailers

Sl. No.	Opinion	No. of Respondents	Per cent
1.	Yes	874	76.7
2.	No	266	23.3
	Total	**1140**	**100.0**

Training to the Customers for Handling New Products

It is observed from Table 6.27 that 22.7 per cent of the respondents opined that the retail shops gave training for handling the new products and the remaining 77.3 per cent of the respondents opined that the retail shops did not give any training for handling the new products. It is concluded from the analysis that majority of the respondents opined that the retail shops did not give any training for handling the new products.

Table 6.27: Training to the Customers for Handling New Products

Sl. No.	Opinion	No. of Respondents	Per cent
1.	Yes	259	22.7
2.	No	881	77.3
	Total	**1140**	**100.0**

Customers Feedback on After Sales Services by Retailers

It is identified from Table 6.28 that 42.1 per cent of the respondents opined as very good towards after sales services, 35.0 per cent of the respondents opined as good towards after sales services, 17.9 per cent of the respondents opined as medium towards after sales services, 4.6 per cent of the respondents opined as poor towards after sales services and remaining 0.4 per cent of the respondents opined as very poor towards after sales services. It is concluded from the analysis that majority of the respondents opined as very good towards after sales services.

Table 6.28: Customers Feedback on After Sales Services by Retailers

Sl. No.	Opinion about Feedback	No. of Respondents	Per cent
1.	Very good	480	42.1
2.	Good	399	35.0
3.	Medium	204	17.9
4.	Poor	53	4.6
5.	Very poor	4	0.4
	Total	**1140**	**100.0**

Feedback on Repurchasing Behaviour

It is noted from Table 6.29 that 89.8 per cent of the respondents opined that they will go to the same shop for repurchasing, 9.1 per cent of the respondents opined that they will change the shop for repurchasing and the remaining 1.1 per cent of the respondents opined that they will change the products when repurchasing. It is concluded from the analysis that majority of the respondents opined that they will go to the same shop for repurchasing.

Table 6.29: Feedback on Repurchasing Behaviour

Sl. No.	Opinion	No. of Respondents	Per cent
1.	Will go to same shop	1024	89.8
2.	Will change the shop	104	9.1
3.	Will change the products	12	1.1
	Total	**1140**	**100.0**

Response on Defective Items by Retailers

It is identified from Table 6.30 (*See on next page*) that 43.4 per cent of the respondents opined that the retailers will be given another product for defective items, 53.3 per cent of the respondents opined that they will not change the product when it is defective, 2.1 per cent of the respondents opined that the retailers will be repaid the money for defective items and the remaining 1.1 per cent of the respondents opined that the products will be repaired and give back for the defective items. It is concluded from the analysis that majority of the respondents opined that the retailers will be given another product for defective items.

Retailers' Response on Customers Complaint

It is observed from Table 6.31 (*See on next page*) that 11.2 per cent of the respondents opined that the retail shop gave very good response to their complaint, 60.5 per cent of the respondents opined that the retail shop gave good response to their complaint, 18.9 per cent of the respondents opined that the retail shop gave medium response to their complaint and 9.3 per cent of the respondents opined that the retail shop gave poor response to their complaint. It is concluded from the analysis that majority of the respondents opined that the retail shop gave good response to their complaint.

Table 6.30: Response on Defective Items by Retailers

Sl. No.	Opinion	No. of Respondents	Per cent
1.	They will give another product	495	43.4
2.	They will not change the product	608	53.3
3.	They will repay the money	24	2.1
4.	The will repair the product and give it back	13	1.1
	Total	**1140**	**100.0**

Table 6.31: Retailers' Response on Customers Complaint

Sl. No.	Opinion	No. of Respondents	Per cent
1.	Very good	128	11.2
2.	Good	690	60.5
3.	Medium	216	18.9
4.	Poor	106	9.3
5.	Very poor	0	0.0
	Total	**1140**	**100.0**

Hospitality Services by Retailers

It is identified from Table 6.32 that 3.6 per cent of the respondents opined that the retail shop gave very good hospitality, 19.4 per cent of the respondents opined that the retail shop gave good hospitality, 53 per cent of the respondents opined that they had no idea about hospitality services provided by the retailers, 23.3 per cent of the respondents opined that the retail shop gave poor hospitality and the remaining 0.7 per cent of the respondents are opined that the retail shop gave very poor hospitality. It is concluded from the analysis that majority of the respondents opined that they have no idea about hospitality services provided by the retailers.

Table 6.32: Hospitality Services by Retailers

Sl. No.	Opinion	No. of Respondents	Per cent
1.	Very good	41	3.6
2.	Good	221	19.4
3.	No idea	604	53.0
4.	Poor	266	23.3
5.	Very poor	8	0.7
	Total	**1140**	**100.0**

Satisfaction with Retail Store Services

It is noted from Table 6.33 that 85.1 per cent of the respondents are satisfied with the retail shop services and the remaining 14.9 per cent of the respondents are not satisfied with the retail shop services. It is concluded from the analysis that majority of the respondents are satisfied with the retail shop services.

Table 6.33: Satisfaction with Retail Store Services

Sl. No.	Opinion	No. of Respondents	Per cent
1.	Yes	970	85.1
2.	No	170	14.9
	Total	**1140**	**100.0**

Methods Used by the Retailers to Develop Their Relationship with Customers

It is observed from Table 6.34 that 27.8 per cent of the respondents opined that the retailer sent seasonal greetings to develop their relationship, 61.1 per cent of the respondents opined that the retailer sent information about new products through mail and the remaining 11.1 per cent of the respondents opined that the retailer developed their relationship with customers by some other communication method. It is concluded from the analysis that majority of the respondents opined that the retailer sent information about new products through mail.

Table 6.34: Methods Used by the Retailers to Develop Their Relationship with Customers

Sl. No.	Opinion	No. of Respondents	Per cent
1.	Sending seasonal greetings	317	27.8
2.	Information about new products through mail	697	61.1
3.	Others	126	11.1
4.	No Method is followed	0	0
	Total	**1140**	**100.0**

HENRY GARRETT RANKING – ANALYSIS

Reasons for Selecting the Particular Retail Shop

Selecting a retail shop is crucial by different reasons. Among the selected five reasons the respondents select different reasons. Most of the respondents selected the retail shop for 'Product quality' which was ranked first by them with a Garrett score of 76023 points. The respondents selected the retail shops for the second and third reasons 'Availability of the products' and 'Hospitality in service' with a Garrett score of 71673 and 51335 points respectively. The respondents selected the fourth and fifth reasons 'Employees co-operation' and 'Proximity' with a Garrett score of 49772 and 38137 points respectively. It could be found from the above analysis that most of the respondents selected the major reasons 'Product quality' and 'Availability of the products'.

Table 6.35: Reasons for Selecting the Particular Retail Shop

Sl. No.	Reasons	Total Score	Mean Score	Rank
1.	Product quality	76023	66.7	I
2.	Hospitality in service	51335	45.0	III
3.	Employees co-operation	49772	43.7	IV
4.	Proximity	38137	33.5	V
5.	Availability of the products	71673	62.9	II

Customer Expectations in Retail Shop

Table 6.36 shows the expectations from the retail shops by the selected sample respondents. It could be noted from the above analysis that most of the selected sample respondents expected from the retail shop 'Product availability' with Garrett score of 72702 points. The respondents expected the second and third factors 'To maintain the Good relationship with Customers' and 'Effective Salesmen Support' with Garrett scores of 68296 and 61335 points respectively. The respondents expected the fourth and fifth factors 'More response in retailer shop' and 'Payment System in Prompt' with Garrett scores of 58556 and 52188 points respectively. The respondents expected sixth and seventh factors 'Retail store Appearance and out look' and 'Credit purchase' with Garrett scores of 48415 and 35738 points respectively. It could be found from the above analysis that most of the respondents expected from the retail shops 'Product availability' and 'To maintain the Good relationship with Customers'.

Table 6.36: Customer Expectations in Retail Shop

Sl. No.	Expectations	Total Score	Mean Score	Rank
1.	To maintain the Good relationship with Customers	68296	59.9	II
2.	Effective Salesmen Support	61335	53.8	III
3.	More response in retailer shop	58556	51.4	IV
4.	Products availability	72702	63.8	I
5.	Retail store Appearance and out look	48415	42.5	VI
6.	Payment System in Prompt	52188	45.8	V
7.	Credit purchase	35738	31.3	VII

Problems Faced by the Consumers during Product Purchase

Table 6.37 throws light on the problems faced by the selected sample respondents for the services offered by the retailer. It is clear from Table 6.37 that majority of the respondents faced the problem of 'Non-availability of products' which was ranked as first by them with a Garrett scored as 49914 points respectively. The respondents faced the second and third problems 'Poor Response of the employees' and 'Retailers Mis-behaviour' with Garrett scores of 40845 and 46422 points. The fourth and fifth problems 'Price variation in different shops' and 'Lack of knowledge about the new Products' are faced by the respondents with Garrett scores of 37775 and 37485 points respectively. The respondents faced the sixth and seventh problems 'Not providing the free gifts' and 'Salesmen's Mis-representation' with Garrett scores of 36309 and 34476 respectively. The respondents faced the eight and ninth problems 'Unable to find the expiry date of products' and 'Lack of parking facility' with Garrett scores of 29152 and 24222 points respectively. It is concluded from the above analysis that most of the respondents faced the major problems 'Non availability of products' and 'Poor Response of the employees'.

Table 6.37: Problems Faced by the Consumers during Product Purchase

Sl. No.	Problems	Total Score	Mean Score	Rank
1.	Non-Availability of products	49914	66.73	I
2.	Poor response of the employees	40845	54.61	II
3.	Lack of knowledge about the new products	37485	50.11	V
4.	Not providing the free gifts	36309	48.54	VI
5.	Salesmen's mis-representation	34476	46.09	VII
6.	Retailers mis-behaviour	46422	62.06	III
7.	Price variation in different shops	37775	50.50	IV
8.	Unable to find the expiry date of products	29152	38.97	VIII
9.	Lack of parking facility	24222	32.38	IX

Age and Level of Satisfaction

It could be observed from Table 6.38 (*see on next page*)that the level of satisfaction perceived by the respondents below 30 years age group ranged between 86 and 125 with an average of 101.58. The level of satisfaction for 31-40 years age group respondents ranged between 81 and 127 with an average of 116.15. On the other hand, above 40 years age group respondents' level of satisfaction ranged between 86 and 125 with an average of 112.67. From the analysis it is identified that the maximum level of satisfaction perceived by the respondents belonged to 31-40 years age group.

Age and Level of Satisfaction (Two-Way Table)

To determine the degree of association between age of the respondents and level of satisfaction in utilizing Fast

Moving Consumer products, a two-way table was prepared and is presented in Table 6.39.

Table 6.38: Age and Level of Satisfaction

Sl. No.	Age	No. of Respondents	%	Average	Range		S.D
					Min	Max	
1.	Below 30 years	394	34.6	101.58	86.0	125.0	10.42
2.	31-40 years	411	36.1	116.15	81.0	127.0	12.70
3.	Above 40 years	335	29.4	112.67	86.0	125.0	10.75
	Total	**1140**	**100.0**				

Table 6.39: Age and Level of Satisfaction (Two-Way Table)

Sl. No.	Age	Level of Satisfaction			Total
		Low	Medium	High	
1.	Below 30 years	136 (34.5)	213 (54.1)	45 (11.4)	394
2.	31-40 years	69 (16.8)	31 (7.5)	311 (75.7)	411
3.	Above 40 years	44 (13.1)	162 (48.4)	129 (38.5)	335
	Total	**249**	**406**	**485**	**1140**

It is highlighted from Table 6.39 that the percentage of high level of satisfaction is the highest (75.7%) among the respondents of 31-40 years age category and the same is the lowest (11.4%) among the respondents of below 30 years age category. The percentage of medium level of satisfaction is the highest (54.1%) among the respondents of below 30 years age category and the lowest (7.5%) among the respondents of 31-40 years age category. On the other hand, the percentage of low level of satisfaction is the highest (34.5%) among the respondents of below 30 years age category, and the same is the lowest (13.1%) among above 40 years age category respondents.

Age and Level of Satisfaction (Chi-Square Test)

In order to find the relationship between age of the respondents and their level of satisfaction, a chi-square test was employed and the result of the test is shown in Table 6.40.

H_0: There is no significant relationship between age of the respondents and level of satisfaction of the customers with FMCG.

H_1: There is significant relationship between age of the respondents and level of satisfaction of the customers with FMCG.

Table 6.40: Age and Level of Satisfaction (Chi-Square Test)

Factor	Calculated χ^2 Value	D.F	Table Value	Remarks
Age	386.272	4	9.488	Significant at 5% level

It is divulged from the above table that the calculated chi-square value is greater than the table value and the result is significant at 5% level. Hence, the hypothesis, "Age of the respondents and their level of satisfaction are associated" holds good. From the analysis, it is identified that there is a close relationship between age of the respondents and level of satisfaction of the customers with Fast Moving Consumer Goods.

Gender and Level of Satisfaction

It is clear from Table 6.41 that the level of satisfaction among the male respondents ranged between 86 and 127 with an average of 104.74. The level of satisfaction among the female respondents ranged between 81 and 125 with an average of 114.36. From the analysis, it is found that the level of satisfaction was at the maximum in female respondents.

Table 6.41: Gender and Level of Satisfaction

Sl. No.	Gender	No. of Respondents	%	Average	Range		S.D
					Min	Max	
1.	Male	506	44.4	104.74	86.0	127.0	11.65
2.	Female	634	55.6	114.36	81.0	125.0	12.49
	Total	**1140**	**100.0**				

Gender and Level of Satisfaction (Two-Way Table)

With a view to find the degree of association between gender and level of satisfaction, a two-way table was prepared and the details are depicted in Table 6.42.

Table 6.42: Gender and Level of Satisfaction (Two-Way Table)

Sl. No.	Gender	Level of Satisfaction			Total
		Low	Medium	High	
1.	Male	159 (31.4)	276 (54.5)	71 (14.0)	506
2.	Female	90 (14.2)	130 (20.5)	414 (65.3)	634
	Total	**249**	**406**	**485**	**1140**

It is highlighted from the above table that the percentage of high level of satisfaction was the highest (65.3%) among the female respondents and the same was the lowest (14.0%) among the male respondents. The percentage of medium level of satisfaction was the highest (54.5%) among the male respondents and the same was lowest (20.5%) among the female respondents. On the other hand, the percentage of low level of satisfaction was the highest (31.4%) among the male respondents and the same was the lowest (14.2%) among the female respondents.

Gender and Level of Satisfaction (Chi-Square Test)

In order to find the relationship between gender of the respondents and level of satisfaction, a chi-square test was used and the result of the test is shown in Table 6.43.

H_0: There is no significant relationship between Sex of the respondents and level of satisfaction towards the customers.

H_1: There is significant relationship between Sex of the respondents and level of satisfaction towards the customers.

Table 6.43: Gender and Level of Satisfaction (Chi-Square Test)

Factor	Calculated χ^2 Value	D.F	Table Value	Remarks
Gender	303.654	2	5.991	Significant at 5% level

It is suggested from the above table that the calculated chi-square value is greater than the table value and the result is significant at 5% level. Hence, the hypothesis, "sex of the respondents and their level of satisfaction are associated" holds good. From the analysis, it is identified that there is a close relationship between sex of the respondents and level of satisfaction towards the customers.

Qualification and Level of Satisfaction

It could be observed from Table 6.44 that the level of satisfaction among the respondents having school level education ranged between 88 and 125 with an average of 105.70 followed by the level of satisfaction among the respondents having UG level education ranged between 86 and 127 with an average of 111.61. The level of satisfaction among the respondents having PG level education ranged between 89 and 125 with an average of 109.83. On the other hand, the level of satisfaction among the professionals that ranged between 81 and 123 with an average of 109.18. From the analysis, it is observed that the maximum level of satisfaction among the respondents with U.G. qualification.

Table 6.44: Qualification and Level of Satisfaction

Sl. No.	Qualification	No. of Respondents	%	Average	Range		S.D
					Min	Max	
1.	School level	197	17.3	105.70	88.0	125.0	10.87
2.	UG	655	57.5	111.61	86.0	127.0	13.74
3.	PG	208	18.2	109.83	89.0	125.0	10.47
4.	Professional	80	7.0	109.18	81.0	123.0	15.36
	Total	**1140**	**100.0**				

Qualification and Level of Satisfaction (Two-Way Table)

With a view to find the degree of association between qualifications of the respondents and level of satisfaction, a two-way table was prepared and the details are exhibited in Table 6.45 (*See on next page*).

It is observed form Table 6.45 that the percentage of high level of satisfaction towards the customers was the highest (55.4%) among the respondents with UG level education and the same was the lowest (4.6%) among the school level respondents. The percentage of medium level of satisfaction was the highest (72.6%) among the school level qualified respondents and the same was lowest (15.0%) among the professionals. The percentage of low level of satisfaction was the highest (32.5%) among the professionals and the same was the lowest (9.6%) among the PG level qualified respondents.

Table 6.45: Qualification and Level of Satisfaction (Two-Way Table)

Sl. No.	Qualifications	Level of Satisfaction			Total
		Low	Medium	High	
1.	School level	45 (22.8)	143 (72.6)	9 (4.6)	197
2.	UG	158 (24.1)	134 (20.5)	363 (55.4)	655
3.	PG	20 (9.6)	117 (56.3)	71 (34.1)	208
4.	Professional	26 (32.5)	12 (15.0)	42 (52.5)	80
	Total	**249**	**406**	**485**	**1140**

Qualification and Level of Satisfaction (Chi-Square Test)

With a view to find relationship between educational qualifications of the respondents and level of satisfaction, a chi-square test was employed and the result of the test is shown in Table 6.46.

H_0: There is no significant relationship between Educational Qualifications of the respondents and level of satisfaction of the customers towards FMCG.

H_1: There is significant relationship between Educational Qualifications of the respondents and level of satisfaction of the customers towards FMCG.

Table 6.46: Educational Qualifications and Level of Satisfaction (Chi-Square Test)

Factor	Calculated □² Value	D.F	Table Value	Remarks
Educational Qualifications	269.956	6	15.592	Significant at 5% level

It is highlighted from Table 6.46 that the calculated chi-square value is greater than the table value and the result is significant at 5% level. Hence, the hypothesis, "Qualification of the respondents and their level of satisfaction are associated" holds good. From the analysis, it is identified that there is a close relationship between qualification of the respondents and level of satisfaction towards the customers.

Occupation and Level of Satisfaction

It is depicted form Table 6.47 that the level of satisfaction among the govt. employees ranged between 65 and 125 with an average of 108.55, followed by the level of satisfaction among the respondents doing business which ranged between 86 and 127 with an average of 113.57. The range of housewives' level of satisfaction ranged between 89 and 125 with an average of 98.87, whereas the level of satisfaction among the professionals ranged between 81 and 125 with an average of 115.81. The range of student's level of satisfaction ranged between 86 and 124 with an average of 99.29. On the other hand, the level of satisfaction among the respondents of other occupation ranged between 89 and 125 with an average of 113.15. From the analysis it is inferred that the maximum level of satisfaction was among the professional customers.

Table 6.47: Occupation and Level of Satisfaction

Sl. No.	Occupation	No. of Respondents	%	Average	Range		S.D
					Min	Max	
1.	Govt. Employee	65	5.7	108.55	95.0	125.0	12.28
2.	Business	549	48.2	113.57	86.0	127.0	11.91
3.	House wife	143	12.5	98.87	89.0	125.0	8.90
4.	Professional	137	12.0	115.81	81.0	125.0	13.40
5.	Student	123	10.8	99.29	86.0	124.0	8.96
6.	Others	123	10.8	113.15	89.0	125.0	11.47
	Total	**1140**	**100.0**				

Occupation and Level of Satisfaction (Two-Way Table)

With a view to find the degree of association between occupation of the respondents and level of satisfaction, a two-way table was prepared and the details are presented in Table 6.48.

Table 6.48: Occupation and Level of Satisfaction (Two-Way Table)

Sl. No.	Occupation	Level of Satisfaction			Total
		Low	Medium	High	
1.	Govt. Employee	23 (35.4)	25 (38.5)	17 (26.2)	65
2.	Business	82 (14.9)	188 (34.2)	279 (50.8)	549
3.	House wife	63 (44.1)	70 (49.0)	10 (7.0)	143
4.	Professional	31 (22.6)	20 (14.6)	86 (62.8)	137
5.	Student	36 (29.3)	73 (59.3)	14 (11.4)	123
6.	Others	14 (11.4)	30 (24.4)	79 (64.2)	123
	Total	**249**	**406**	**485**	**1140**

It is found from Table 6.48 that the percentage of high level of satisfaction was the highest (62.8%) among the professionals and the same was lowest (7%) among the respondents of housewives. The percentage of medium level of satisfaction was the highest (59.3%) among the students and the same was lowest (14.6) among the professionals. The percentage of low level of satisfaction was the highest (44.1%) among the housewives and the same was the lowest (11.4%) among the customers of others.

Occupation and Level of Satisfaction (Chi-Square Test)

In order to find the relationship between occupation of the respondents and level of satisfaction, a chi-square test was employed and the result of the test is shown in Table 6.49.

H_0: There is no significant relationship between Occupation of the respondents and level of satisfaction of the customers.

H_1: There is significant relationship between Occupation of the respondents and level of satisfaction of the customers.

Table 6.49: Occupation and Level of Satisfaction (Chi-Square Test)

Factor	Calculated χ^2 Value	D.F Value	Table	Remarks
Occupation	217.704	10	18.307	Significant at 5% level

It is inferred from Table 6.49 that the calculated chi-square value is greater than the table value and the result is significant at 5% level. Hence, the hypothesis, "Occupation of the respondents and their level of satisfaction are associated" holds good. From the analysis, it is identified that there is a close relationship between occupation of the respondents and level of satisfaction towards the customers.

Monthly Income and Level of Satisfaction

It is observed from Table 6.50 that the level of satisfaction among respondents whose income was below Rs.5000 ranged between 88 and 125 with an average of 107.51 followed by the level of satisfaction among the Rs.5,000-10,000 income earners which ranged between 86 and 127 with an average of 111.58. The level of satisfaction among the Rs.10,001-20,000 income earners ranged between 81 and 125 with an average of 113.48. On the other hand, the range of above Rs.20,000 income earners' level of satisfaction was between 89 and 125 with an average of 102.39. From the analysis it is inferred that the maximum level of satisfaction was among the respondents in the income group of Rs.10,001-20,000.

Table 6.50: Monthly Income and Level of Satisfaction

Sl. No.	Monthly Income	No. of Respondents	%	Average	Range		S.D
					Min	Max	
1.	Below Rs. 5000	150	13.2	107.51	88.0	125.0	9.06
2.	Rs. 5000-10000	518	45.4	111.58	86.0	127.0	13.61
3.	Rs. 10001-20000	293	25.7	113.48	81.0	125.0	13.18
4.	Above Rs. 20000	179	15.7	102.39	89.0	125.0	10.19
	Total	**1140**	**100.0**				

Monthly Income and Level of Satisfaction (Two-Way Table)

With a view to determine the degree of association between income of the respondents and their level of satisfaction, a two-way table was framed and is shown in Table 6.51.

Table 6.51: Monthly Income and Level of Satisfaction (Two-Way Table)

Sl. No.	Monthly Income	Level of Satisfaction			Total
		Low	Medium	High	
1.	Below Rs. 5000	12 (8.0)	114 (76.0)	24 (16.0)	150
2.	Rs. 5000-10000	120 (23.2)	114 (22.0)	284 (54.8)	518
3.	Rs. 10001-20000	50 (17.1)	88 (30.0)	155 (52.9)	293
4.	Above Rs. 20000	67 (37.4)	90 (50.3)	22 (12.3)	179
	Total	**249**	**406**	**485**	**1140**

It could be seen from the above table that the percentage of high level of satisfaction was the highest (54.8%) among the respondents earning Rs. 5,000-10,000 per month and the same was the lowest (12.3%) among the respondents of earning above Rs. 20,000 per month. The percentage of medium level of satisfaction was the highest (76.0%) among the respondents earning below Rs. 5,000 income per month and the same was the lowest (22%) among the respondents earning Rs. 5,000-10,000 per month. The percentage of low level of satisfaction was the highest (37.4%) among the respondents' who belonged to the income group of above Rs. 20,000 and the same was the lowest (8.0) among the respondents in the below Rs. 5,000 income group.

Monthly Income and Level of Satisfaction (Chi-Square Test)

In order to find the relationship between income of the respondents and level of satisfaction, a Chi-square test was employed and the result is shown in Table 6.52.

H_0: There is no significant relationship between Monthly Income of the respondents and level of satisfaction of the customers towards products.

H_1: There is significant relationship between Monthly Income of the respondents and level of satisfaction of the customers towards products.

Table 6.52: Monthly Income and Level of Satisfaction (Chi-Square Test)

Factor	Calculated c^2 Value	D.F	Table Value	Remarks
Monthly Income	234.650	6	12.592	Significant at 5% level

It is inferred from Table 6.52 that the calculated chi-square value is greater than the table value and the result is significant at 5% level. Hence, the hypothesis, "Monthly income of the respondents and their level of satisfaction are associated" holds well. From the analysis, it is identified that there is a close relationship between monthly income of the respondents and level of satisfaction of the customers.

Marital Status and Level of Satisfaction

It is obvious from Table 6.53 that the level of satisfaction among the married respondents ranged between 81 and 127 with an average of 114.22 whereas the unmarried respondents' level of satisfaction ranged between 86 and 125 with an average of 100.05. From the analysis it is observed that the maximum level of satisfaction was among the married category respondents.

Table 6.53: Marital Status and Level of Satisfaction

Sl. No.	Marital Status	No. of Respondents	%	Average	Range		S.D
					Min	Max	
1.	Married	808	70.9	114.22	81.0	127.0	11.95
2.	Unmarried	332	29.1	100.05	86.0	125.0	9.66
	Total	**1140**	**100.0**				

Marital Status and Level of Satisfaction (Two-Way Table)

With a view to find the degree of association between marital status of the respondents and level of satisfaction, a two-way table was prepared and is displayed in the Table 6.54.

Table 6.54: Marital Status and Level of Satisfaction (Two-Way Table)

Sl. No.	Marital Status	Level of Satisfaction			Total
		Low	Medium	High	
1.	Married	119 (14.7)	234 (29.0)	455 (56.3)	808
2.	Unmarried	130 (39.2)	172 (51.8)	30 (9.0)	332
	Total	**249**	**406**	**485**	**1140**

It is inferred from Table 6.54 that the percentage of high level of satisfaction is the highest (56.3%) among the married respondents and the same is the lowest (9.0%) among the respondents of unmarried category. The percentage of medium level of satisfaction is the highest (51.8%) among the unmarried category respondents and the lowest (29.0%) among the married category respondents. On the other hand, the percentage of low level of satisfaction is the highest (39.2%) among the unmarried category respondents and the same is lowest (14.7%) among the married category respondents.

In order to find the relationship between marital status of the respondents and their level of satisfaction, a Chi-square test was employed and the result is shown in Table 6.55.

H_0: There is no significant relationship between Marital Status of the respondents and level of satisfaction of the customers.

H_1: There is significant relationship between Marital Status of the respondents and level of satisfaction of the customers.

Table 6.55: Marital Status and Level of Satisfaction (Chi-Square Test)

Factor	Calculated χ^2 Value	D.F	Table Value	Remarks
Marital Status	222.399	2	5.991	Significant at 5% level

It is disclosed from Table 6.55 that the calculated chi-square value is greater than the table value and the result is significant at 5% level. Hence, the hypothesis, "Marital status of the respondents and their level of satisfaction are associated" holds good. From the analysis, it is identified that there is a close relationship between marital status of the respondents and level of satisfaction towards the customers.

Number of Members in the Family and Level of Satisfaction

Table 6.56 indicates that the level of satisfaction among the respondents having below 3 members in their family ranged between 81 and 125 with an average of 110. The level of satisfaction of the respondents who have 3-6 members in their family ranged between 86 and 127 with an average of 109.34. The level of satisfaction among the respondents of having above 6 members in their family that ranged between 95 and 124 with an average of 116.95. The analysis clearly proves that the maximum level of satisfaction in utilizing FMC products was among the respondent with large families.

Table 6.56: Number of Members in the Family and Level of Satisfaction

Sl. No.	No. of Members	No. of Respondents	%	Average	Range		S.D
					Min	Max	
1.	Below 3 members	203	17.8	110.00	81.0	125.0	12.95
2.	3-6 members	842	73.9	109.34	86.0	127.0	13.21
3.	Above 6 members	95	8.3	116.95	95.0	124.0	9.09
	Total	**1140**	**100.0**				

Number of Members in the Family and Level of Satisfaction (Two-Way Table)

In order to find the degree of association between number of members in the family and level of satisfaction, a two-way table was formulated and the results are given in Table 6.57. (*See on next page*)

It is identified from Table 6.57 that the percentage of high level of satisfaction was the highest (73.7) among the respondents having above 6 members in their family and the same was the lowest (23.2) among below 3 members in their family. The percentage of medium level of satisfaction was the highest (59.1) among the respondents having below 3 members in their family and the same was the lowest (17.9) among above 6 members in their family. The percentage of low level of satisfaction was the highest (24.3) among the respondents of 3-6 members in their family and the same was the lowest (8.4) among the respondents having above 6 members in their family.

Table 6.57: Number of Members in the Family and Level of Satisfaction (Two-Way Table)

Sl. No.	No. of Members	Level of Satisfaction			Total
		Low	Medium	High	
1.	Below 3 members	36 (17.7)	120 (59.1)	47 (23.2)	203
2.	3-6 members (24.3)	205 (31.9)	269 (43.7)	368	842
3.	Above 6 members (8.4)	8 (17.9)	17 (73.7)	70	95
	Total	**249**	**406**	**485**	**1140**

Number of Members in the Family and Level of Satisfaction (Chi-Square Test)

In order to find the relationship between number of members in the family and level of satisfaction, a chi-square test was employed and the result of the test is shown in Table 6.58.

H_0: There is no significant relationship between number of members in the family and level of satisfaction of the customers.

H_1: There is significant relationship between Number of members in the family and level of satisfaction of the customers.

Table 6.58: Number of Members in the Family and Level of Satisfaction (Chi-Square Test)

Factor	Calculated χ^2 Value	D.F	Table Value	Remarks
No. of members	94.713	4	9.488	Significant at 5% level

It is explained from Table 6.58 that the calculated chi-square value is greater than the table value and the result is significant at 5% level. Hence, the hypothesis, "Number of members in the family and their level of satisfaction are associated" holds good. From the analysis, it is identified that there is a close relationship between number of members in the family and level of satisfaction of customers towards FMCG.

Awareness and Level of Satisfaction

It is identified from Table 6.59 that the level of satisfaction among the respondents having low level of awareness ranged between 98 and 127 with an average of 119.42. The level of satisfaction among the respondents having medium level of awareness that ranged between 81 and 125 with an average of 45.1. The range of high level awareness ranged between 89 and 122 with an average of 106.17. From the analysis it is inferred that the maximum level of satisfaction was found among the respondents who had low level of awareness.

Table 6.59: Awareness and Level of Satisfaction

Sl. No.	Awareness	No. of Respondents	%	Average	Range		S.D
					Min	Max	
1.	Low	318	27.9	119.42	98.0	127.0	7.39
2.	Medium	492	43.2	106.69	81.0	125.0	13.82
3.	High	330	28.9	106.17	89.0	122.0	11.53
	Total	**1140**	**100.0**				

Awareness and Level of Satisfaction (Two-Way Table)

With a view to find the degree of association between awareness of the respondents and level of satisfaction, a two-way table was framed and is shown in Table 6.60.

Table 6.60: Awareness and Level of Satisfaction (Two-Way Table)

Sl. No.	Awareness	Level of Satisfaction			Total
		Low	Medium	High	
1.	Low	10 (31.1)	60 (18.9)	248 (78.0)	318
2.	Medium	152 (30.9)	169 (34.3)	171 (34.8)	492
3.	High	87 (26.4)	177 (53.6)	66 (20.0)	330
	Total	**249**	**406**	**485**	**1140**

It is depicted from Table 6.60 that the percentage of high level of satisfaction was the highest (78%) among the respondents having low level of awareness and the same was the lowest (20%) among the respondents having high level awareness. The percentage of medium level of satisfaction was the highest (53.6%) among the respondents having high level of awareness and the same was the lowest (18.9%) among the respondents having low level of awareness. On the other hand the percentage of low level of satisfaction was the highest (31.1%) among the respondents having low level of awareness and the same was the lowest (26.4%) among the respondents having high level of awareness.

Awareness and Level of Satisfaction (Chi-Square Test)

In order to find the relationship between awareness of the respondents and their level of satisfaction, a chi-squared test was employed and the result of the test is shown in Table 6.61.

H_0: There is no significant relationship between awareness of the respondents and their level of satisfaction.

H_1: There is significant relationship between awareness of the respondents and their level of satisfaction.

Table 6.61: Awareness and Level of Satisfaction (Chi-Square Test)

Factor	Calculated χ^2 Value	D.F	Table Value	Remarks
Awareness	268.137	4	9.488	Significant at 5% level

It is pin-pointed from the above table that the calculated chi-square value is greater than the table value and the result is significant at 5% level. Hence, the hypothesis "Awareness of the respondents and their level of satisfaction are associated" holds goods. It is concluded from the analysis that there is a close relationship between awareness of the respondents and their level of satisfaction.

Period of Relationship with the Shop and Level of Satisfaction

It could be understood from Table 6.62 that the respondents having a relationship of up to 5 years with the shop have perceived a level of satisfaction which ranged between 86 and 125 with an average of 104.74 whereas the level of satisfaction of the respondents having a relationship of 6-8 years with the shop ranged between 86 and 127 with an average of 114.48. The respondents with 9-10 years of relationship have perceived a level of satisfaction which ranged between 96 and 116 with an average of 106.12. On the other hand, the level of satisfaction perceived by the respondents having a relationship of above 10 years ranged between 81 and 116 with an average of 100.15. Thus the table reveals that the respondents with 6-8 years of relationship exhibit the maximum level of satisfaction.

Table 6.62: Period of Relationship with the Shop and Level of Satisfaction

Sl. No.	Period	No. of Respondents	%	Average	Range		S.D
					Min	Max	
1.	Upto 5 years	325	28.5	104.74	86.0	125.0	13.43
2.	6-8 years	594	52.1	114.48	86.0	127.0	11.77
3.	9-10 years	98	8.6	106.12	96.0	116.0	6.69
4.	Above 10 years	123	10.8	100.15	81.0	116.0	8.54
	Total	**1140**	**100.0**				

Period of Relationship with the Shop and Level of Satisfaction (Two-Way Table)

With a view to find the degree of association between the period of relationship with the shop and the level of satisfaction perceived by the respondents, a two-way table was prepared and the same is shown in Table 6.63.

Table 6.63: Period of Relationship with the Shop and Level of Satisfaction (Two-Way Table)

Sl. No.	Period	Level of Satisfaction			Total
		Low	Medium	High	
1.	Up to 5 years	125 (38.5)	110 (33.8)	90 (27.7)	325
2.	6-8 years	77 (13.0)	192 (32.3)	325 (54.7)	594
3.	9-10 years	13 (13.3)	35 (35.7)	50 (51.0)	98
4.	Above 10 years	34 (27.6)	69 (56.1)	20 (13.0)	123
	Total	**249**	**406**	**485**	**1140**

It is seen from the above table that the percentage of high level of satisfaction perceived by the respondents is the highest (54.7%) among the respondents with 6-8 years' relationship with the shop and the same was the lowest

(13%) among the respondents who had above 10 years' relationship. The percentage of medium level of satisfaction was the highest (56.1) among the respondents with above 10 years relationship with the shop and the lowest (32.3%) among the respondents possessing a relationship of 6-8 years. On the other hand, the percentage of low level of satisfaction was the highest (38.5%) among the respondents of up to 5 years relationship and the lowest (13%) among the respondents of 6-8 years of relationship with the shop.

Periods of Relationship with the Shop and Level of Satisfaction (Chi-Square Test)

In order to find the relationship between the period of relationship with the shop and level of satisfaction, a chi-square test was employed and the result of the test is shown in Table 6.64.

H_O: There is no significant relationship between periods of relationship with the shop and level of satisfaction.

H_1: There is significant relationship between periods of relationship with the shop and level of satisfaction.

Table 6.64: Periods of Relationship with the Shop and Level of Satisfaction (Chi-Square Test)

Factor	Calculated χ^2 Value	D.F	Table Value	Remarks
Period	143.473	6	12.592	Significant at 5% level

It is witnessed from Table 6.64 that the calculated chi-square value is greater than the table value and the result is significant at 5% level. Hence, the hypothesis "Period of relationship with the shop and level of satisfaction are associated" holds goods. It is concluded from the analysis that there is a close relationship between period of relationship with the shop and level of satisfaction.

FACTOR ANALYSIS

A 'factor' is an underlying dimension that accounts for several observed variables. There can be one or more factors, depending upon the nature of the study and the number of variables involved in it. 'Factor-loadings' are those values which explain how closely the variables are related to each one of the factors discovered. 'Communality', symbolized as h^2, shows how much of each variable is accounted for by the underlying factor taken together. A high value of communality means that not much of the variable is left over after whatever the factors represent is taken into consideration. It is worked out in respect of each variable as under:

h^2 of the ith variable = (ith factor loading of factor A) + (ith factor loading of factor B) + . . .

When the sum of squared values of factor loadings relating to a factor is taken, then such sum is referred to as 'Eigen Value' or latent root. Eigen value indicates the relative importance of each factor in accounting for the particular set of variables being analyzed.

When Eigen values of all factors are totaled, the resulting value is termed as the total sum of squares. This value, when divided by the number of variables, results in an index that shows how the particular solution accounts for what all the variables taken together represent.

'Rotation', in the context of factor analysis, is something like staining a microscope slide. Just as different stains on it reveal different structures in the tissue, different rotations reveal different structures in the data. Though different rotations give results that appear to be entirely different, but from a statistical point of view, all results are taken as equal, none superior or inferior to others. However, from the standpoint of making sense of the results of factor analysis, one must select the right rotation. If the factors are independent, orthogonal rotation is done and if the factors are correlated, an oblique rotation is made. Communality for each variable will remain undisturbed regardless of rotation but the Eigen values will change as a result of rotation.

'Factor score' represents the degree to which each respondent gets high on the group of items that load high on each factor. Factor scores can help to explain what the factors mean. With such scores, several other multivariate analyses can be performed.

Principal-Component Method of Factor Analysis

Principal-components method (or simply P.C. method) of factor analysis, developed by H. Hotelling, seeks to maximize the sum of squared loadings of each factor extracted in turn. Accordingly PC factor explains more variance than the loadings would obtain from any other method of factoring.

The aim of the principal-components method is the construction out of a given set of variables X_j's $(j = 1, 2, \ldots, k)$, of new variables (p_i), called principal components which are linear combinations of the X_s.

$$p_1 = a_{11}X_1 + a_{12}X_2 + \ldots + a_{1k}X_k$$
$$p_2 = a_{21}X_1 + a_{22}X_2 + \ldots + a_{2k}X_k$$
$$. \quad . \quad . \quad . \quad . \quad .$$
$$. \quad . \quad . \quad . \quad . \quad .$$
$$. \quad . \quad . \quad . \quad . \quad .$$
$$p_k = a_{k1}X_1 + a_{k2}X_2 + \ldots + a_{kk}X_k$$

The method is being applied mostly by using the standardized variables, i.e.,

$$z_j = \left(X_j - \bar{X}_j\right)^2 / \sigma_j.$$

The σ_{ij}'s are called loadings and are worked out in such a way that the extracted principal components satisfy two conditions: (i) principal components are uncorrelated (orthogonal) and (ii) the first principal component (p_1) has the maximum variance, the second principal component (p_2) has the next maximum variance and so on.

'Communality', symbolized as h^2, shows how much of each variable is accounted for by the underlying factor taken together. A high value of communality means that not much of the variable is left over after whatever the factors represent is taken into consideration. It is worked out in respect of each variable as under:

h^2 of the *i*th variable = (*i*th factor loading of factor A) + (*i*th factor loading of factor B) + . . .

By using the above formula, communalities have been extracted from the available variables by using principal-component method with the help of normalizing factor. Table 6.65 (*See on next page*) shows the variables with the corresponding extraction communality factor value.

Table 6.66 revealed that the extraction has been undertaken by using principal-component method and the initial Eigen values are formulated from the communalities table and the same has been developed as extraction sums of squared loadings with percentage of variance and the relative cumulative percentage. From the initial Eigen values and the extraction sums of squared loadings values, the rotation sums of squared loadings has been formulated and shown in Table 6.66. (*See on page 186*)

Table 6.65: Variable with Extracted Community Factor Value–Satisfaction

Variables	Initial	Extraction
Factor 1	1	0.726
Factor 2	1	0.794
Factor 3	1	0.782
Factor 4	1	0.892
Factor 5	1	0.772
Factor 6	1	0.735
Factor 7	1	0.632
Factor 8	1	0.805
Factor 9	1	0.792
Factor 10	1	0.790
Factor 11	1	0.813
Factor 12	1	0.677
Factor 13	1	0.658
Factor 14	1	0.781
Factor 15	1	0.845
Factor 16	1	0.780
Factor 17	1	0.845
Factor 18	1	0.833
Factor 19	1	0.894
Factor 20	1	0.880
Factor 21	1	0.802
Factor 22	1	0.830

Where,

Factor 1	–	Retailers Behaviour
Factor 2	–	Retailer's information about the products
Factor 3	–	Customer – Retailers relations
Factor 4	–	Product delivery
Factor 5	–	Quality Maintenance
Factor 6	–	Product varieties
Factor 7	–	Response
Factor 8	–	Availability of the products
Factor 9	–	Friendly approach
Factor 10	–	Payment System
Factor 11	–	Delivery System
Factor 12	–	Bills passing
Factor 13	–	Product varieties
Factor 14	–	Different sizes
Factor 15	–	Package styles
Factor 16	–	Products availability
Factor 17	–	Information about new products
Factor 18	–	Information about free products
Factor 19	–	Price of the products
Factor 20	–	Price matches with products
Factor 21	–	Price discounts for old products
Factor 22	–	Price allowances for new products

Table 6.66: Total Variance–Level of Satisfaction

Component	Initial Eigen values			Extraction Sums of Squared Loadings			Rotation Sums of Squared Loadings		
	Total	% of Variance	Cumulative %	Total	% of Variance	Cumulative %	Total	% of Variance	Cumulative %
1	2	3	4	5	6	7	8	9	10
1.	13.212	60.053	60.053	13.212	60.053	60.053	7.741	35.185	35.185
2.	1.707	7.760	67.813	1.707	7.760	67.813	5.373	24.424	59.609
3.	1.376	6.252	74.066	1.376	6.252	74.066	2.653	12.057	71.667
4.	1.066	4.846	78.912	1.066	4.846	78.912	1.594	7.245	78.912
5.	0.720	3.271	82.183						
6.	0.663	3.015	85.198						
7.	0.564	2.566	87.764						
8.	0.441	2.003	89.766						
9.	0.401	1.822	91.588						
10.	0.339	1.539	93.128						

(Contd...)

1	2	3	4	5	6	7	8	9	10
11.	0.299	1.359	94.487						
12.	0.243	1.106	95.593						
13.	0.230	1.044	96.637						
14.	0.183	0.832	97.469						
15.	0.130	0.590	98.059						
16.	0.119	0.541	98.600						
17.	0.088	0.399	98.999						
18.	0.069	0.313	99.313						
19.	0.065	0.297	99.609						
20.	0.040	0.180	99.789						
21.	0.034	0.152	99.942						
22.	0.013	0.058	100.000						

Extraction Method: Principal Component Analysis.

The extraction process has been carried out by using principal-component method, and it is found that from the rotation sums of squared loadings and the total sum of twenty two variables has been extracted and the same has been grouped into four components which have Eigen value of more than one. It ranges from component No. 1 to component No. 4 with the cumulative percentage from 60.053 per cent to 78.912 per cent. The percentage of variance ranges from 60.053 per cent to 4.846 per cent. For the fourth component of initial Eigen values, the total, percentage of variance and the cumulative percentage values are 1.066 per cent, 4.846 per cent and 78.912 per cent respectively. The extracted sum of squared loadings for the same was 1.066 per cent, 4.846 per cent and 78.912 per cent respectively. The rotation sum of squared loadings for the above was 1.594 per cent, 7.245 per cent and 78.912 per cent respectively.

From the analysis, it is inferred that the factor analysis has been supported upto 78.912 per cent in this study. This is an excellent result and made the study reliable to the analysis.

Table 6.67 has been formulated by using 'principal-component method' for extraction of variables into components and Varimax with Kaiser Normalization has been undergone by using 'rotation method'. All the twenty two variables have been grouped into four components and each component consists of sets of factors and the analysis has been made to identify the influence of one variable over another.

It is observed from the Table 6.67 that the following are the results extracted from the rotation component matrix among 22 variables. Among the 22 variables the Component factor 1 consisted of eleven variables which have high influence with one another. They are variable no. 1, 6, 7, 8, 9, 10, 12, 13, 19, 20 and 21. Component factor 2 consisted of seven variables which have high influence with one another and they are 2, 4, 5, 11, 14, 15 and16.

Table 6.67: Rotated Component Matrix[a] – Level of Satisfaction

Variable No.	Component			
	1	2	3	4
Factor 1	0.719			
Factor 2		0.609		
Factor 3				0.587
Factor 4		0.798		
Factor 5		0.629		
Factor 6	0.605			
Factor 7	0.623			
Factor 8	0.650			
Factor 9	0.798			
Factor 10	0.773			
Factor 11		0.699		
Factor 12	0.582			
Factor 13	0.588			
Factor 14		0.624		
Factor 15		0.721		
Factor 16		0.800		
Factor 17				0.919
Factor 18			0.896	
Factor 19	0.914			
Factor 20	0.822			
Factor 21	0.834			
Factor 22			0.700	

a. Rotation converged in 7 iterations.

Extraction Method: Principal Component Analysis

Rotation Method: Varimax with Kaiser Normalization

Component factor 3 has two closely influencing variables and the numbers are 18 and 22. Finally component factor 4 has two high influencing variables and the variable numbers are 3 and 17 respectively.

From the factor analysis, it has been identified that all the twenty two factors are very much closely associated with one another and the same has been analyzed by using factor analysis and the influence of one factor with another has been tested and the same has succeeded in measuring the correlation between the particular variable and the factor with 78.912 percent reliability and the factor analysis supported the study.

Therefore, it is observed from the factor analysis that out of 22 variables only six variables are showing significant contribution. They are Products availability, Information about new products, Price of the products, Price matches with products, Price discounts for old products and Payment system. These factors are very much closely associated with one another.

DISCRIMINANT FUNCTION ANALYSIS (DFA)

The level of satisfaction among the customers varies in the different stages of experiencing services. In the study area out of 1140 respondents divided into two groups, low level of satisfier and the other is high level of satisfier by the selected respondents. How do the respondents in one group differ from the other is studied with the help of Discriminant function analysis. For the purpose of the study nine variables were selected:

1. Age
2. Gender
3. Educational Qualifications
4. Occupation
5. Monthly Income level
6. Marital Status
7. Family size
8. Level of Awareness
9. Period of using service
   (With respect to level of performance)

The DFA attempts to construct a function with these and other variables so that the respondents belonging to these 2 groups are differentiated at the maximum. The linear combination of variables is known as Discriminant Function and its parameters are called Discriminant function coefficients. In constructing this DF all the variables which contribute more to differentiate these two groups are examined.

Mahalanobis minimum D^2 method is based on the generalized squared Euclidean distance that adjusts for unequal variances in the variables. The major advantage of this procedure is that it is computed in the original space of the predictor (independent) variables rather than as a collapsed version which is used in the other method.

Generally, all the variables selected will not contribute to explain the maximum discriminatory power of the function. So a selection rule is applied based on certain criteria to include those variables which best discriminate. Stepwise selection method was applied in constructing DF which selects one variable at a time to be included in the function. Before entering into the functions the variables are examined for inclusion in the function.

The variables which could have maximum D^2 value, if entered into the function are selected for inclusion in the function. Once entered any variable already in the equation is again considered for removal based on certain removal criteria. Likewise, at each step the next best discriminating variable is selected and included in the function and any variable already included in the function is considered for removal based on the selection and removal criteria respectively.

DISCRIMINANT ANALYSIS FOR THE PROBLEM UNDER STUDY

Since DFA involved classification problem also to ascertain the efficiency of the DFA all the variables which satisfy the entry and removal criteria were entered into the function. Normally the criterion used to select the variables for inclusion in the function is minimum F to enter into the equation (i.e.) F statistic calculated for the qualified variable to enter into the function is fixed as ≥ 1.

Similarly, any variable entered in the equation will be removed from the function if F statistic for the variable calculated is <1. The 2 groups are defined as:

Group 1 – Low level satisfier

Group 2 – High level satisfier

The mean and standard deviation for these groups and for the entire samples are given for each variable considered in the analysis.

Table 6.68: Between Low and High Satisfier Groups – Group Means

No.	Variables	Low	High	Total
1.	Age	2.243	1.647	1.948
2.	Gender	1.738	1.369	1.556
3.	Educational Qualification	2.170	2.130	2.150
4.	Occupation	2.941	3.190	3.064
5.	Monthly Income level	2.373	2.508	2.439
6.	Marital Status	1.066	1.522	1.291
7.	Family size	1.929	1.881	1.905
8.	Level of Awareness	1.880	1.988	1.933
9.	Period of using service	1.750	2.277	2.011

The overall step wise D.F.A. results after all significant discriminators have been included in the estimation of discriminated function are given in the Table 6.70.

Table 6.69: Between Low and High Satisfier Groups – Group Standard Deviation

No.	Variables	Low	High	Total
1.	Age	0.629	0.840	0.798
2.	Gender	0.440	0.483	0.497
3.	Educational Qualification	0.716	0.847	0.784
4.	Occupation	1.556	1.417	1.493
5.	Monthly Income level	0.670	1.096	0.908
6.	Marital Status	0.248	0.500	0.455
7.	Family size	0.556	0.440	0.503
8.	Level of Awareness	0.435	1.086	0.825
9.	Period of using service	0.799	0.598	0.754

Table 6.70: Summary Table Between Low and High Satisfier Groups

Step	Variable entered	Wilk's lambda	Minimum D^2	Significance
1.	Marital Status	0.748	1.347	*
2.	Level of Awareness	0.677	1.902	*
3.	Period of using	0.670	1.970	*
4.	Gender	0.664	2.021	*

* Significant at 1% level.

The summary table indicates that the variable marital status is entered in step 1, level of awareness is entered in step 2, period of using is entered in step 3 and variable gender is entered in the step 4. The variables marital status, level of awareness, period of using and gender are significant at 1% level. All the variables are significant discriminators' based on their Wilk's Lambda and D^2 value. The multivariate aspect of the model is given in Table 6.71.

Table 6.71: Canonical Discriminant Function (Between Low and High Satisfier Groups)

Canonical correlation	Wilks Lambda	Chi-square	D.F.	Sig
0.580	0.664	465.214	4	Significant at 1% level

The canonical correlation is 0.580 when squared, that is 33.6% of the variance in the Discriminant group can be accounted for by this model, Wilk's Lambda and chi-square value suggest that D.F. is significant at 1% level.

The variables given above are identified finally by the D.F.A. as the eligible discriminating variables. Based on the selected variables the corresponding D.F. coefficients are calculated. They are given in the following Table 6.72.

Table 6.72: Discriminant Function Coefficients (Between Low and High Satisfier Groups)

Marital Status	1.931
Level of Awareness	0.702
Period of using services	0.244
Gender	-0.392
Constant	-3.767

$$
\begin{aligned}
Z = & -3.767 \\
& + 1.931\,(\text{Marital status}) \\
& + 0.702\,(\text{Level of Awareness}) \\
& + 0.244\,(\text{Period of using}) \\
& - 0.392\,(\text{Gender})
\end{aligned}
$$

Using this DF coefficients and variables discrimi-nating scores for 2 groups are found out and are called group centroids or group means.

For Low satisfier (Z_1) it is – 0.702

For High satisfier (Z_2) it is + 0.720

Discriminating factor is the weighted average of Z_1 and Z_2.

$$\text{i.e. } Z = \frac{577 \times Z_1 + 563 \times Z_2}{577 + 563}$$

If it is represented diagrammatically it will be

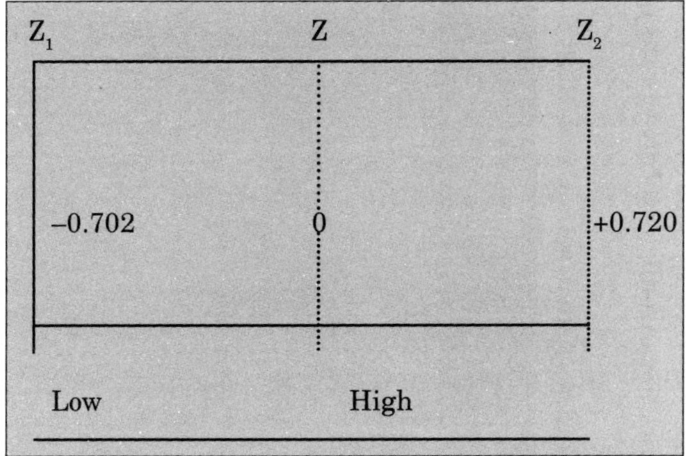

Thus to classify any respondent as to low and high satisfier the Z score for the respondent is found out by using the equation.

If the score found out for any respondent is Z_0 and if the value is >Z (i.e. $Z_0 > Z$) then it is classified into high satisfier and if $Z_0 < Z$ then (i.e. $Z_0 < Z$) it is classified in the low satisfier.

Now the questions remain to be answered are:

1. How efficient are the discriminating variables in the D.F.A.?
2. How efficient the D.F. itself is?

The first question cannot be answered directly; however, the discriminating power or the contribution of each variable to the function can sufficiently answer the question. For this consider the Table 6.73.

Table 6.73: Relative Discriminating Index (Between Low and High Satisfier Groups)

Variables	Group 1 Mean X_1	Group 2 Mean X_2	Unstandardized dic. Coeff. (kj)	I_j = ABS (K_j) Mean $(X_{jo} - x_{ji})$	$R_j = I_j$/sum Ij j*100
Marital Status	1.066	1.522	1.931	1.49	66.9
Level of Awareness	1.880	1.988	0.702	0.36	16.4
Period of using	1.750	2.277	0.244	0.12	5.4
Gender	1.738	1.369	-0.392	0.25	11.3
Total				**2.22**	**100.000**

For each variable the respective D.F. co-efficient, its mean for each group and R_j are given. R_j called relative discriminating index is calculated from the discriminant function coefficient and group means. R_j tells us how much each variable is contributing (%) to the function. By looking at this column we find that marital status is maximum discriminating variable and year of establishment is the least discriminating variable.

The second question is answered by reclassifying the already grouped individuals into low and high using the D.F. (Z) defined in the equation. This reclassification is called predictor group membership. In short, the efficiency of the D.F. is how correctly it predicts the respondents into respective groups.

Table 6.74: Classification Results (Between Low and High Satisfier Group)

Actual Group	No. of Cases	Predicted Group Membership	
		Group I	Group II
Group I (Low Satisfier)	577	479 (83.0%)	98 (17.0%)
Group 2 (High Satisfier)	563	202 (35.9%)	17.0 (64.1%)

Per cent of grouped cases correctly classified: 73.7%.

Table 6.74 gives the results of the reclassification. The function, using the variables selected in the analysis classified 73.7 per cent of the cases correctly in the respective groups.

Discriminate function analysis was applied to the respondents based on the low and high satisfiers. The following factors significantly discriminate the two user groups. They are:

1. Gender
2. Marital Status

3. Period of using services and
4. Level of Awareness.

MULTIPLE REGRESSION ANALYSIS

In the following analysis, the relationship between the level of satisfaction among the customers and nine independent factors was studied. It was found that out of nine, seven factors were closely associated with the level of satisfaction by the selected sample respondents.

The selected nine independent factors are:

1. Age
2. Gender
3. Educational Qualifications
4. Occupation
5. Monthly Income level
6. Marital Status
7. Family size
8. Level of Awareness
9. Period of using service

In order to measure the interdependence of independent factors and their level of satisfaction, the results were subjected to multiple regression analysis. The results of multiple regression analysis are shown in Table 6.75.

Table 6.75 indicates that the co-efficient of period of using service is positively associated with the level of customers' satisfaction. On the other hand, the co-efficient of Age, Gender, Educational Qualifications, Monthly Income level, Marital Status and Family size are negatively associated. Further, it indicates that the contribution of period of using service is statistically significant implying that their influence on level of satisfaction is stronger than that of other variables.

Table 6.75: Multiple Regression Analysis

Sl. No.	Variables	Unstandardized coefficients		Standardized coefficients	T	Sig.
		B	Std. Error	Beta		
	(Constant)	2.828	0.055		51.221	
1.	Age	–0.350	0.011	–0.614	–32.001	1%
2.	Gender	–0.304	0.018	–0.333	–16.927	1%
3.	Educational Qualifications	–0.058	0.012	–0.100	–5.034	1%
4.	Occupation	–0.005	0.006	–0.017	–0.857	NS
5.	Monthly Income level	–0.056	0.011	–0.111	–4.939	1%
6.	Marital Status	–0.075	0.012	–0.129	–6.479	1%
7.	Family size	–0.019	0.009	–0.034	–2.086	5%
8.	Level of Awareness	–0.008	0.014	–0.013	–0.548	NS
9.	Period of using service	0.059	0.015	0.066	3.839	1%

R-Value	R^2 - Value	Degree of freedom – V_1	Degree of freedom – V_2	F Value	Significance
0.839	0.703	9	1130	297.6	1% Level

Multiple regression analysis results shows that out of nine variables selected, only four variables are closely associated with the level of customers' satisfaction. The multiple linear components are found statistically the good fit as R^2 is 0.703. It shows that the independent variables contribute about 70.3 per cent on the variation in the level of satisfaction of customers are statistically significant at 1% level and 5% level respectively.

Summary of Findings Suggestions and Conclusion

INTRODUCTION

The study is aimed at measuring the Customer Relationship Management (CRM) practised by the retailers with special reference to Fast Moving Consumer Goods (FMCG) in Erode District, and the problems faced by both Retailers and Customers during CRM practices in the study area. For this purpose, 510 samples of retailers were selected at random and the samples of 1140 customers were selected from Erode District. Field survey technique was employed to collect the first-hand information from the sample respondents of both retailers and the customers. Questionnaire was the main tool employed to collect the primary data. The data thus collected were arranged in to simple tabular forms and appropriate statistical tools were used for data analysis. Based on this analysis, interpretations were made systematically. In this chapter, an attempt was made to recapitulate the key findings and conclusion. Based on these findings, a few suggestions have also been made.

FINDINGS

CRM Practices and Problems Faced by FMCG Retailers in the Study Area

1. It could be noted from the analysis, that majority of the retailers have established their retail shop for

6-10 years. Among them, the average year of experience was 7 to 9 years leading with only one retail outlet.

2. Majority of the retailers opined that their Customers Expectations are fulfilled and expressed their opinion as good. Simultaneously, the same comment of good was expressed for the relationship maintained by the retailers with the customers.
3. Most of the retailers complemented that Customers Behaviour is very good while selecting the products in the retail store. Further, they pinpointed that they did not face any problem with customers.
4. It is divulged from the analysis that majority of the retailers opined that the customers' awareness level is good for new products.
5. It is revealed from the analysis that majority of the retailers (64.1%) did not give any training to their customers. And it is identified from the analysis that majority of the retailers find customer behaviour good.
6. It is observed from the analysis that majority of the retailers expressed that the customers usually purchase in a week, and they purchase the products by cash mode.
7. From the analysis, majority (61.8%) of the retailers opined that some customers give full payment at the time of purchasing the products. In general, the customers buy low priced products.
8. It is identified from the analysis that majority of the retailers opined that the customers' awareness on advertisements for products are high.
9. It is noticed from the analysis, 98.6 per cent of the retailers opined about their customers feeling that their expected products are available in the retail shop.

10. It is confirmed from the analysis that majority (85.9%) of the retailers opined that their customers enquiry on requirements by direct contact. Advertisement is the main medium to induce their requirement, which was witnessed with 81.8 per cent.

11. It is evident from the analysis that majority of the retailers opined that the TV advertisements mostly create a center of attention.

12. It is observed from the analysis that majority of the customers suing questions against the products' life time.

13. Majority (87.3%) of the retailers opined that the retailers do not provide any hospitality services in their shop separately.

14. It is obtained from the analysis that few of the retailers maintain their customers' details in their database, and the retailers use this database to maintain a personal touch through sending seasonal greetings to their customers.

15. It is clear from the analysis that most of the customers are 'Home makers' which ranked first by them with Garrett scores of 35325 points.

16. It could be noted from the analysis that majority of the retailers opined among the FMCG products, the customers preferred to purchase 'Soaps and cosmetics' and 'Teeth cleaning products' as their first choice. Further, it was learnt that the main reasons for selecting the retail shops due to availability of product at low price.

17. The results of the analysis reveals that the retailers having 15 years of experience in retail business have perceived maximum level of satisfaction. It is also witnessed from the ANOVA test that there is a significant difference between year of establishment and level of satisfaction.

18. It was perceived on level of satisfaction was the highest among the retailers those who have 4-6 years of experience. Further, ANOVA test also found that there is a significant difference between experience of the retailers and their level of satisfaction.

19. From the analysis, it is identified that the retailers having more number of outlets have perceived the maximum level of satisfaction. Further, ANOVA test also concluded that there is significant difference between number of retail outlets and level of satisfaction.

20. From the analysis it is identified that the maximum level of satisfaction perceived by retailers through credit purchase system. And also the percentage of highest level of satisfaction perceived by the retailers was the highest among the retailers who purchased through same credit mode. It is found from ANOVA analysis that there is no significant difference between mode of purchase and level of satisfaction.

Customers Opinion on CRM Practices by the Retailers of FMCG Products

1. It is clear from the analysis that Majority of the customers belong to 30-40 years of age group. Among them, Majority of customers are females in the selected sample of 1140 respondents.

2. It is revealed from the analysis that majority of the customers are educated up to UG level. Further, majority of the customers are engaged in business.

3. It is noted from the analysis that majority of the customers are earning income between Rs. 5000-10000 per month. Majority of the customers (70.9%) are married.

4. It is observed from the analysis that majority of the customers are having 3 to 6 members (73.9%) in their

family. Further, it is witnessed that majority of the customers maintain relationship with two shops.

5. It is found from the analysis that majority of the customers are aware about the retail shops for 3 to 5 years. Further, majority of the customers became aware about the retail shop through relatives. And also, the customers became aware about the retail shop through Posters and Pamphlets.

6. It is identified from the analysis that majority of the customers are aware about the retail shop is not only with FMCG products, but also dealing with some other products.

7. It is stated from the analysis that majority of the Customers pointed that the Retailers behaviour is very good in the retail shop. And majority of the customers (96.7%) are satisfied with the services offered by the retailers. Further, it is divulged that majority of the customers are satisfied with the availability of the products in the retail shops.

8. It is witnessed from the analysis that majority of the customers opined that the retailers give very good response towards services provided by them in the retail shop.

9. It is stated from the analysis that majority of the customers opined that the Product varieties available in the retail shop are very good in the retail shop. Further, that majority of the customers realized that price matches with the products in the selected retail store.

10. It is noted from the analysis, Majority of the customers opined that price discounts are good in the retail shop. Further, Mostly customers (99.6 per cent) purchase the products by cash payment.

11. It is observed from the analysis that majority of the customers are satisfied with the present advertisement. Further, the customers stated newspaper media is the best choice for advertisement.
12. It is proved from the analysis that majority of the customers faced some problems by utilizing the services offered by the retail shops like free gifts, offers, retailers response, price discounts etc. Further, most of the customers faced the major problems 'Non availability of products' and 'Poor response of the employees' in the retail shop.
13. It is observed from the analysis that majority of the customers opined that the retailers response for their complaints was good. But, it is identified that majority the retailers do not change if any defective items purchased were submitted for replacement.
14. It is identified from the analysis that 94.6 per cent of the customers are satisfied with the retailers' performance in the market. And majority of the customers (76.7%) felt that their expectations were fulfilled by the retailers.
15. It is stated from the analysis that majority (77.3%) of the customers said that the retailers do not give any training for handling the new products.
16. It is witnessed from the analysis that majority of the customers opined as very good towards after sales services for household items. Further, it is witnessed that majority of the customers (89.8%) intended to go the same shop for repurchasing.
17. From the analysis, Majority of the customers said that they had no idea about hospitality services provided by the retailers. This reflects about the customers receive no hospitality in the retail store.

18. 85.1 per cent of the customers are satisfied with the retail shop services. Further, it is witnessed that majority of the retailers sent information about new products through mail.

19. Most of the customers select FMCG because of the 'quality of the products' and on the basis of the 'Availability of the products'. Further, it was found that most of the customers expect 'Product availability' and maintenance of 'Good relationship with the Customers'.

20. It is learnt from the analysis that the maximum level of satisfaction in using FMCG products was identified among the customers belonged to 31-40 years age group. Further, the chi-square test also proved that there is a close relationship between age of the customers and level of satisfaction towards the customers.

21. It is clear from the analysis, that the maximum level of satisfaction with the products was perceived by the female customers. Further, the chi-square (x^2) test also proved that there is a close relationship between sex of the customers and level of satisfaction towards the customers.

22. From the analysis, it is observed that the maximum level of satisfaction identified in consuming products among the customers with U.G Qualification. The chi-square test also proved that there is a close relationship between qualification of the customers and level of satisfaction of the customers.

23. It is depicted form the analysis that the maximum level of satisfaction in using the goods was identified among the Professional customers. Further, the chi-square test also proved that there is a close relationship between occupation of the customers and level of satisfaction of the customers.

24. It is observed from the analysis that the maximum level of satisfaction was identified among the customers in the income group of Rs.10,001-20,000. Further, the chi-square test also proved that there is a close relationship between monthly income of the customers and level of satisfaction of the customers while purchasing FMCG in the retail store.
25. From the analysis it is disclosed that the maximum level of satisfaction was found among the 'married' category customers. Further, the chi-square test also has shown that there is significant relationship between marital status of the customers and the level of satisfaction of the products purchased by the customers.
26. It is clearly proved that the maximum level of satisfaction in utilizing FMC Goods was among the customers with large families i.e. above 6 members. Further, the chi-square test also found that there is a close relationship between number of members in the family and level of satisfaction of customers towards the products.
27. It is identified from the analysis that the maximum level of satisfaction was found among the customers who had low level of awareness about the product details. Further it cleared from the chi-square test that there is a close relationship between awareness of the customers and their level of satisfaction.
28. From the analysis, it is evident that the customers with 6-8 years of relationship with the retail shops of their choice exhibit the maximum level of satisfaction. Further it is witnessed from the chi-square test that there is a close relationship between the period of relationship with the shops and the level of satisfaction of the customers.
29. It is observed from the factor analysis that out of twenty two variables only six variables are showing

significant contribution. They are Products availability, Information about new products, Price of the products, Price matches with products, Price discounts for old products and Payment system. These factors are very much closely associated with one another.

30. Discriminant function analysis was also applied to the customers based on the low and high satisfiers. The following factors significantly discriminate the two user groups. They are Gender, Marital Status, Period of using services and Level of Awareness.

31. The multiple regression analysis results shows that out of nine variables selected, only four variables are closely associated with the level of customers' satisfaction. The multiple linear components are found statistically the good fit as R^2 is 0.703. It shows that the independent variables contribute about 70.3 per cent on the variation in the level of satisfaction of customers are statistically significant at 1% level and 5% level respectively.

SUGGESTIONS

Following are the suggestions from the findings for the further improvement of Customer Relationship Management system by the retailers of FMCG in Erode District.

1. In order to ensure a lasting and non-lasting customer relationship, the retailers should have a customer database, customer analysis, customer profiling, customer segmentation and campaign management. It should also take steps for evolving the configuration of products suitable and are being preferred by the consumers. The company should ensure proper invoicing and maintenance a customer care wing and self service facilities.

2. From the finding, more number of customers give due attention on low priced FMCG products and they do

not seek quality of products much in the retail shop. This may be persuaded by retailers for giving the importance of quality of the products to the customers.

3. Some of the retailers do not have much information on new products in their retail shop. Therefore, such kind of information can be obtained by them from the FMCG manufacturers. This may help the retailers for representing more information to their customers.

4. The Retailers face the problems with customers when they ask for different varieties of products then and there come up in the market and their persistent demand for free gifts which are normally given only for a limited period, current retail price for FMCG, availability of newly advertised products, price off and seasonal offers for products, etc. This may be considered by the retailers as very urging factors for maintaining good relationship with customers.

5. Most of the retailers do not give any training for their customers about using newly launched products like, Shampoos, Soaps, Face creams, Toilet cleaners, Different types of Tooth brushes matching with teethes, etc. These things can be demonstrated by the retailers in their store itself while opening a small R&D cell. It will boost the customers' opinion on increasing the image of the retail store in their mind.

6. The retailers do not provide much about hospitality services like water facilities, sitting facilities, entertainment cell, providing Tea during evening time etc. This may be concentrated by the retailers for further maintaining relationship with their real customers.

7. Nowadays, more numbers of retailers do not maintain the customers' data base through their Information Technology system. Customer data base may give the information about their purchasing patterns, kind of

products they regularly choose in the retail shop. This is very much important to maintain customer data base which may enhance the strong relationship with their customers.

8. Some of Retailers do not send any seasonal greeting or offers to their regular customers due to improper maintenance of customer data base. Therefore, data base may also support for sending seasonal greetings like birthday greetings, wedding anniversary, etc. and some offers during festivals and also greetings on new products information. This will remind the customers about their regular retail shop and its image.

9. Most of the Consumers feel there are no good parking facilities for their Two-wheelers and four-wheelers near the retail store. This may be considered by the FMCG Retailers in order to increase rapport with the consumers.

10. Sometimes, the FMCG consumers do not have an awareness of New Products and Services and availability of free gifts for existing products. This may be intimated to them by the retailers through Display board in front of the cash counter and Hoardings or pamphlets.

11. Strategies to attract new customers like mailing invitations on offers, discounts, new arrivals, approaches through marketing executives, concession in tariff like VAT, MRP and value added services like door delivery may be implemented. Some other strategies which can be followed by the retailers to retain the existing customers through prompt delivery, regular touch with customers, compliments on every occasion, delivery with proper bills, sending proper invoice with thanks letter, etc.

12. From the analysis, it is observed that most of the customers are females than males. Therefore retailers

may appoint the well qualified and well-mannered sales persons to sell the products in the retail shop.

13. Majority of the customers maintain the relationship with two shops. Through, this result, sometimes the customers may be diverted for buying the products from one shop to another. Therefore the retailers could foresee the customers' expectations and their satisfaction towards goods and services in their retail store.

14. More numbers of new customers get awareness about the retail store services through their relatives. So, the retailers should treat their customers as their boss.

15. Majority of the customers are satisfied with the services offered by the retail shops during their purchase in the retail store and the availability of the existing and new products, and these may also be continued in future. This may lead to increase the market share of the Products.

16. Few Advertisements do not clearly deliver the message to the customers and thereby deprive the customers in taking decisions for buying such products found in the retail shop. Therefore, retailers can discuss this factor with the manufacturers to give innovative, simple and easy understandable advertisements through customers' expected media like Newspapers, Television, Posters and Pamphlets.

17. Many customers face the problems like retailers' response, return or exchange of defective items and information on newly advertised products during the purchase. In order to maintain Customer Relationship Management, retailers should take immediate decisions in it.

18. Some of the customers felt that their expectations were not fulfilled by the retailers. Therefore, retailers can

fix the permanent suggestion boxes in front of the retail shop to get the feedback from the customers about opinion, expectations, and attitudes of the retail shop concerned and also their likes and dislikes of the products available with the retailers as well as in the market.

19. Many numbers of customers face the problems of Retailers' mis-behaviour, Price variation in different shops and Lack of knowledge about the new products. Necessary action can be taken by the retailers and the manufacturers in this connection.

CONCLUSION

Customer relationship Management (CRM) plays an important role in the retail market of Fast Moving Consumer Goods (FMCG). In Indian economy, there are varieties of Retail Stores including organized and unorganized sector that plays a crucial role in enhancing the economy of the country through its huge market share. While analyzing the world level Retailing, India occupies the 5th place for Retail Marketing and FMCG Products. In today's world, the scope and use of Fast Moving Consumer Goods have expanded to such an extent that it is now claimed that this is considered to be the world's largest Industry with high rate of employee strength, and that which bring in a lot of revenue to the countries.

Erode District, which is a business and industrial area and is famous for Oil Industry, Cotton and Textile Industry, Turmeric Industry, Sugar Industry, and emerging of Retail outlets of FMCG products showed the hallmark in the per-capita income which is high and it contributes considerably to the revenue of the state income, Rs. 3296.09 crores. This is one of the main trading centers in India. There are 1050 FMCG retail stores and many numbers of buyers in Erode District. Hence, the FMCG products are having fast movement in all the areas in this district. Therefore, Retailers have started having increased avenues for selling, like Mega shopping Malls, Departmental stores, etc. In the current situation, most of the retailers of FMCG fulfill the needs and wants of the customers, and they seriously view customers' expectations and opinion; satisfactory level of customers and the problems faced by them in doing business while the customers find difficulties in selecting the products in their selected retail stores.

The production and consumption of these selected products have witnessed a significant transformation in the past 15 years. The customers will be benefited while Retailers concentrate on CRM practice with latest technology. As for as retailers of Fast Moving Consumer Goods (FMCG) concerned, there is moderate level of CRM practices and the retailers interaction with the customers through traditional approach. Few retailers scientifically have not practised the CRM system in Erode District.

In this book, there are major problems faced by both the retailers and customers like maintenance of customer data base, information on free goods, parking facilities, customers' expectations, awareness on new products, adequate training on using new products, etc. The suggested recommendations may be governed by the retailers to create good rapport with their customers for increasing further strength of CRM system among Retailers and the Customers.

To enhance profitability and customers' satisfaction in Marketing sector, the retailers must focus on implementing Customer Relationship Management (CRM) strategies like customer database, customer retention, data mining and tracking system that aim to seek, gather and store right information, validate and share it throughout the entire organization that could offer solutions. Necessary attention should be given to individual customers in order to attract and retain them. India's FMCG sector faces stiff challenges in increasing the efficiency in several of its sub-sectors for improving the technology in Retailing and its process. Extension of such improvements to Consumers and Retailers apart from reformation of policy in the marketing of FMCG domestically and internationally, will increase the benefits of both retailers and customers. All the players need to join together with the Government in a creative partnership to enhance efficiency and equity in this important sector.

Bibliography

BOOKS

Bagawathi and Pillai R.S.N, "Modern Marketing Management – Principles and Practices", S. Chand Publications, New Delhi, 2000, pp. 3-5.

Batra K. Satish and Shhkazmi, "Consumer Behaviour Text and Cases", Excell Books Publications, New Delhi, 2004, p.66.

Blakwel D. Roger, Paul W. Miniard and James F. Engel, "Consumer Behaviour", Vikas Publishing House, New Delhi, 2002, pp. 22-25.

Cohen Dorothy, "Consumer Behaviour", Random House Business Division, Delhi, 1998, pp. 45-54.

Dune M. Patrick, Robert R Lusch and David A Groffith, "Retailing", Thomson Learning, USA, 2005, pp. 4-5.

Evans R. Joel, Barry Berman, "Marketing in the 21st Century", Biztantra, New Delhi, 2003, pp. 50-51.

Jobber David, "Principles and Practice of Marketing", Tata McGraw Hill, New Delhi, 1998, pp. 36-40.

Kardes R. Frank, "Consumer Behaviour and Managerial Decision Making", Pearson Education, New Delhi, 2007, p. 25.

Kotler Phillip, "Marketing Management", Pearson Education, New Delhi, 2003, p. 237.

McKenna. R, "Relationship Marketing: Successful Strategies for the Age of the Customers", Addison Wesley Publishing Company, 1991, pp. 105-109.

Nair R. Suja, "Consumer Behaviour in Indian Perspective", Himalaya Publishing House, New Delhi, 2001, pp. 314-317.

Palmer Adrian, "Introduction to Marketing Theory and Practice", Tata McGraw-Hill, New Delhi, 2005, pp. 36-40.

Payne A, Jagdish. N, Sheth and Atul Parvatiyar, 'Relationship Marketing – The UK Perspective: Handbook of Relationship Marketing", Sage Publications, UK, 2000, pp. 39-68.

Prasad R.S, "Understanding CRM - Present and Future", ICFAI University Press, Hyderabad, 2005, pp.34-40 & pp. 111-113.

Riezebos R, "Brand Management: A Theoretical and Practical Approach", Pearson Education, Harlow, 2003, pp. 66-72.

Saxena Rajan, "Marketing Management", Tata McGraw-Hill, New Delhi, 2002, p. 32.

Schiffman G. Leon and Leslie Lazar Kanuk, "Consumer Behaviour", Prentice Hall of India, New Delhi, 2007, p. 526.

Semnik J. Richard, "Promotion and Integrated Communications", Thomson Learning, USA, 2005, pp. 45-47.

Shainesh G and Jagdish N. Sheth, "Customer Relationship Management – A Strategic Perspective", Macmillan India Limited, Mumbai, 2007, pp. 23-27.

Sherlakar S.A, "Marketing Management", Himalaya Publishing House, New Delhi, 1997, pp. 149-152.

Sheth J.N, Parvatiyar. A and Shainesh.G, "Conceptual Framework of Customer Relationship in CRM – Emerging Concepts, Tools and Applications", Tata McGraw-Hill, New Delhi, 2000, pp. 3-25.

Simon Knox, Stan Maklan and Joe Peppard, "Customer Relationship Management", Elsevier India Private Limited, New Delhi, 2008, pp. 17-24.

William. G Zikmund, Raymond Mc-Leod.Jr and Faye W. Gilbert, "Customer Relationship Management", John Wiley & Sons: Wiley Students Edition, Singapore, 2004, pp. 88-92.

Wind, Jerry and Vijay Mahajan, "Convergence Marketing: Strategies for Reaching the New Hybrid Consumer", Prentice-Hall, Harlow, UK, 2002, pp. 320-326.

Xavier M.J, "Strategic Marketing for Developing Sustainable Competitive Advantage", Response Books, New Delhi, 2005, pp. 7-9.

Zeithmal A.Valarie and Mary Jo Bitner, "Services Marketing – Integrating Customer Focus Across the Firm", Tata McGraw-Hill, New Delhi, 2001, pp. 45-50.

Zeng Y.E, H.J.Wen and D.C.Yen, "Customer Relationship Management (CRM) in Business (B2B) e-commerce, Information Management & Computer Security", Thomson Learning, USA, 2003, pp. 39-45.

Zigmund and Amico, "Marketing, Thomson Learning", USA, 2006, pp. 123-125.

JOURNALS AND MAGAZINES

Ajith Kumar, "MARKOR: A Measure of Market Orientation," *Journal of Marketing Research*, 30th November, 1993, pp. 467-477.

Alba, Joseph W, John Lynch, Barton Weitz, Chris Janiszewski, Richard Lutz, Alan Sawyer, and Stacy Wood, "Interactive Home Shopping: Consumer, Retailer, and Manufacturer Incentives to Participate in Electronic Marketplaces," *Journal of Marketing*, 6th July, 1997, pp. 38-53.

Allyn, Bacon.Berry. W.L, Hill. T and Klopmaker. J.E, "Aligning Marketing and Manufacturing Strategies with the Market", *International Journal of Production Research*, Vol. 37, 1999, p. 35-45.

Anderson, Eugene W, Claes Fornell, and Donald R. Lehmann, "Customer Satisfaction, Market Share, and Profitability," *Journal of Marketing*, Vol. 58, July 1994, pp. 53-66.

Anderson J. C and Narus. J.A, "A Model of Distributor Firm and Manufacturer Firm Working Partnerships", *Journal of Marketing,* Vol. 54, 1990, p. 42.

Ansari, Asim and Carl F. Mela, "E-Customization," *Journal of Marketing Research*, Vol. 40, May 2003, pp. 131-45.

Bayus, B.L, "An Analysis of Product Lifetimes in a Technologically Dynamic Industry", *Management Science*, Vol. 44, 1998, p. 763.

Berry, L.L., "Relationship Marketing of Services – Growing Interest & Emerging Perspectives", *Journal of the Academy of Marketing Science*, Feb 1995, pp. 236-245.

Berry, L., Zeithaml, V. and Parasuraman, A, "Five Imperatives for Improving Service Quality", *Sloan Management Review*, Vol. 31, 1990, p. 29.

Boulding, William, Ajay Kalra and Richard Staelin, "The Quality Double Whammy," *Marketing Science*, Vol. 18 (4), 1999, pp. 463-84.

Boyd, J, "IT Says No to CRM Integration", *Internet Week*, issue. 886, 2001, p. 1.

Broadbent, M, & Weill. P, "The Implications of Information Technology Infrastructure for Business Process Redesign", *MIS Quarterly,* Vol. 23, 1999, p. 159.

Brown, J, "NCR Blames CRM Failures on Infrastructure", *Computing Canada,* Vol. 27, 2001, p. 17.

Cholewka, K, "CRM: The Failures are Your Fault", *Sales and Marketing Management*, Vol. 36, January 2002, pp. 33-42.

Coffee, P., "In Pursuit of a CRM Process", *eWeek*, Harper Business Press, New York, 2002, p. 24.

Corner. I and Hinton, M, "Customer Relationship Management Systems: Implementation Risks and Relationship Dynamics", *Qualitative Market Research*, Vol. 5, 2002, p. 139.

Daft, R.L and Huber, G.P "How Organizations Learn: A Communication Framework", *Research in Organizational Behaviour,* Vol. 5, 1987, pp. 1-36.

Day, George S. and C.Van den Bulte "Superiority in Customer Relationship Management: Consequences for Competitive Advantage and Performance", Wharton School of Business, *University of Pennsylvania*, 2002, pp. 30.

Degeratu, Alexandru, Arvind Rangaswamy, and Jianan Wu, "Consumer Choice Behaviour in Online and Traditional Supermarkets: The Effects of Brand Name, Price, and Other Search Attributes," *International Journal of Research in Marketing*, vol.17, March 2000, pp.55–79.

Dwyer, F.R., Paul H. Schurr and Sejo Oh, "Developing Buyer – Seller Relationships", *Journal of Marketing*, Vol. 51, April 1987, pp. 11-27.

Ferguson, R.B., "Improving Data Visibility", *eWeek*, Vol. 19, 2002, p. 21.

Fornell and Claes, "A National Customer Satisfaction Barometer:The Swedish Experience," *Journal of Marketing*, Vol. 56, January 1992, pp. 6–21.

Gupta, I., "Managing Customers – The Joy Factor", *Business World*, 26 June 2000, pp.22-28.

Gupta, Sunil, Donald R. Lehmann, and Jennifer Ames Stuart, "Valuing Customers," *Journal of Marketing Research*, Vol. 40, February 2004, pp. 7-18.

Hahn, J and Kauffman. R.J, "Evaluating Web Site Performance in Internet-Based Selling from a Business Value Perspective", *Information and Decision Sciences*, University of Minnesota, 2001, pp. 23-32.

Hahn, J, Kauffman.R. J and Park. J, "Designing for ROI: Toward a Value-Driven Discipline for E-Commerce Systems Design", *Information and Decision Sciences*, University of Minnesota, 2002, pp. 27.

Homburg, Christian and Christian Pflesser, "A Multiple-Layer Model of Market-Oriented Organizational Culture: Measurement Issues and Performance Outcomes," *Journal of Marketing Research*, Vol. 37, November 2000, pp. 449-462.

Irwin, Julie R. and Gary H. McClelland, "Misleading Heuristics and Moderated Multiple Regression Models," *Journal of Marketing Research*, Vol. 38, February 2001, pp. 100-109.

Jacqueline Thomas and V. Kumar, "Balancing Customer Acquisition and Retention Resources to Maximize Customer Profitability," *Journal of Marketing*, Vol. 69, January 2005, pp. 63-79.

Jayachandran, Satish, Subhash Sharma, Peter Kaufman and Pushkala Raman, "The Role of Relational Information Processes and Technology Use in Customer Relationship Management," *Journal of Marketing*, Vol. 69, October 2005, pp. 177-92.

Kline, H "CRM: Overcoming the Infrastructure Hurdle", *Business Communications Review*, July 2001, pp. 45-54.

Mason, Charlotte H. and William D. Perreault (1991), "Collinearity, Power, and Interpretation of Multiple Regression Analysis," *Journal of Marketing Research*, 28 (August), pp. 268-280.

Mithas, Sunil, M.S. Krishnan and Claes Fornell, "Why Do Customer Relationship Management Applications Affect Customer Satisfaction?" *Journal of Marketing*, Vol. 69, October 2005, pp. 3-9.

Plakoyiannaki, E. and N. Tzokas, "Customer Relationship Management: A Capabilities Portfolio Perspective" *Journal of Database Marketing,* Vol. 9, 2002, pp. 201-209.

Reibstein and David. J, "What Attracts Customers to Online Stores, and What Keeps Them Coming Back?" *Journal of the Academy of Marketing Science*, Vol. 30, 2002, pp. 65-73.

Reinartz, Weiner, Manfred Krafft, and Wayne D. Hoyer, "The CRM Process: Its Measurement and Impact on Performance," *Journal of Marketing Research*, Vol. 41, August 2004, pp. 293-305.

Rigby, D.K, F.F. Reichheld and P. Schefter, "Avoid the Four Perils of CRM", *Harvard Business Review,* Vol. 101, February 2002, pp. 79-88.

Rust, Roland. T, Katherine. C, Lemon and Valarie Zeithaml "Return on Marketing: Using Customer Equity to Focus Marketing Strategy," *Journal of Marketing*, Vol. 68, January 2004, pp. 109-127.

Sanal Mazvancheryl, "Customer Satisfaction and Shareholder Value", *Journal of Marketing*, Vol. 68, October 2004, pp. 172-185.

Sirdeshmukh, D. J. Singh and B. Sabol, "Consumer Trust, Value, and Loyalty in Relational Exchanges", *Journal of Marketing,* Vol. 66, 2002, pp. 15.

Srivastava, Rajendra K, Tasadduq Shervani and Liam Fahey, "Market-Based Assets and Shareholder Value:

A Framework for Analysis", *Journal of Marketing*, Vol. 62, January 1998, pp. 2-18.

Sureshchandar, G.S., C. Rajendran, and T.J. Kamalanabhan, "Customer Perceptions of Service Quality: A Critique", *Total Quality Management,* Vol. 12, 2001, pp. 11.

Szulanski and Gabriel, "Exploring Internal Stickiness: Impediments to the Transfer of Best Practices within the Firm", *Strategic Management Journal*, Vol. 17 (1), 1996, pp. 27-43.

Tallon, P.P., Kraemer. K.L and Gurbaxani. V, "Executives Perceptions of the Business Value of Information Technology: A Process-Oriented Approach", *Journal of Management Information Systems,* Vol. 16, 2000, p. 145.

Kumar, V., "On the Profitability of Long-Life Customers in a Non-contractual Setting: An Empirical Investigation and Implications for Marketing," *Journal of Marketing*, Vol. 64, October 2000, pp. 17-35.

Zeithaml, Valarie A., "A Dynamic Process Model of Service Quality: From Expectations to Behavioral Intentions," *Journal of Marketing Research*, Vol. 30, February 1993, pp. 7-27.

Venkatesan, Rajkumar and V. Kumar "A Customer Lifetime Value Framework for Customer Selection and Resource Allocation Strategy", *Journal of Marketing*, Vol. 68, October 2004, pp. 106-125.

Zauberman and Gal "The Inter Temporal Dynamics of Consumer Lock-In", *Journal of Consumer Research*, Vol. 30, December 2003, pp. 405-419.

Zutshi and Sudhir, "Relationship Marketing: A Real Marketing Tool in Present Market Conditions", *The Journal of Indian Management and Strategy*, Vol. 8, July-September 2003, pp. 54-63.

Index

GRATER
wooden mixing spoon
ladle
SPOONS
CASSEROLE DISH
SAUCEPAN (POT)
ELECTRIC MIXER
tube
spring form
SPECIAL PANS
BAKING PAN
KNIVES
butter
paring (SHARP)
MIXING BOWL